THE FAMILIES REMEMBER

Cat. No: CP32-89/1-2008E
ISBN: 978-0-660-19779-1

Available through your local bookseller or through
Publishing and Depository Services
Public Works and Government Services Canada
Ottawa, Ontario
KIA OS5

Telephone: (613) 941-5995 or 1 800 635-7943
Fax: (613) 954-5779 or 1 800 565-7757
publications@pwgsc.gc.ca
Internet: www.publications.gc.ca

MGov

Commission of Inquiry
into the Investigation of
the Bombing of Air India
Flight 182

Commission d'enquête relative
aux mesures d'investigation prises
à la suite de l'attentat à la bombe
commis contre le vol 182 d'Air India

The Honourable John C. Major, Q.C.
Commissioner

L'honorable John C. Major, c.r.
Commissaire

December 2007

To Her Excellency
The Governor General in Council

May it please your Excellency:

As Commissioner appointed by Order in Council P.C. 2006-293 issued on
May 1, 2006 pursuant to Part 1 of the *Inquiries Act*, and in accordance with
the Terms of Reference assigned therein, I respectfully submit this first report
entitled "The Families Remember." This report contains personal stories about
many of the victims of the bombing of Air India flight 182 and their families,
as well as the rescuers and Canadian officials who were in Ireland immediately
after the tragedy.

John C. Major
Commissioner

P.O. Box 1298, Station "B", Ottawa, Ontario / C.P. 1298, succursale "B" Ottawa (Ontario)
K1P 5R3
Tel. / Tél. : 613 992-1834   Fax / Télécopieur : 613 995-3506
E-mail: jmajor@majorcomm.ca

Canada

Table of Contents

Introduction

In the evening of June 22, 1985, Air India Flight 182, a Boeing 747 named *Kanishka* took off from Montreal bound for London and later New Delhi. In the early morning of June 23rd it was blown apart from a bomb planted by terrorists in Canada, killing all on board.

Three hundred and twenty-nine passengers and crew died. Of these people, 137 were under 18 and 82 were under 13. This remains the greatest loss of Canadians at the hands of terrorists.

The grief to the families and friends was instant, profound and enduring. Grief is paralyzing in its effect and a challenge to convey in print or speech. *Mark Stagg* met that challenge. He was an officer on the *Laurentian Forest*, among the first ships to arrive at the scene.

Mark Stagg described to the Commission the carnage encountered. The oil-slicked waters of the North Atlantic circled the scene of destruction. Wreckage and broken bodies were scattered over a wide area. He recovered some bodies and parts of others and held the hope that some passengers might have survived. That hope was dashed when he lifted a child fully clothed and unmarked from the sea. He hoped for life but knew at once the child was dead. He described pressing the body to his own cheek and feeling the cold confirmation of death. He never forgot that moment; he lives with it still:

> *The boy in me died that day. I don't recognize this until years later, but I feel the passing. I felt it then and I feel it now, and every day my mind is drawn there. My faith in goodness, and God, and sense and normality died then...*[1]

---

[1] Mark Stagg, speaking before the Commission on September 27, 2006. He was the Third Officer on the *MV Laurentian Forest*, the vessel that carried out recovery operations following the bombing. Today he is the head of training and development for the Maritime and Coastguard Agency, United Kingdom Department of Transport.

In spite of the obvious magnitude of the catastrophe, Canada and Canadians in general did not immediately recognize it as a terrorist attack against Canadians. That acceptance was long in coming. Indeed, the first public appearance by a Canadian prime minister at the memorial service in Ireland did not occur until 2005. A lengthy investigation by the RCMP and a long and thorough trial in British Columbia of two suspects, Ripudaman Singh Malik and Ajaib Singh Bagri, ended in acquittals in 2005, to the disappointment of the families. As of today, the only person convicted in connection with any aspect of the bombing of Flight 182 or the Narita Airport explosion is Inderjit Singh Reyat. (See Annex C for a timeline of key events).

This preliminary report focuses on the human element arising from the bombing — the accompanying suffering of the victims' families, the heroism of the rescuers and the generosity and warmth of the citizens of Cork, Ireland. The enormity of this mass murder may be grasped by attempting to know more about the victims and their grieving survivors.

Prior to Prime Minister Stephen Harper calling this Inquiry, the Honourable Bob Rae, former premier of Ontario, considered whether there were outstanding questions of public interest related to the bombing of the Air India flight that should be answered after 20 years. He examined how the criminal investigation was conducted as well as the findings and recommendations from other investigations. He assessed the transportation and security measures taken by federal departments and agencies since 1985. He also visited family members and others and delivered a helpful report in the fall of 2005. In it he wrote:

> We know the location of the conspiracy that planned the bombings, and the identity of some of the conspirators; we know how the bombs got on two planes; we know the details of the bombs' detonation. We do not need to re-visit these questions. They are clearly established. What we need to know more about is how Canada assessed the threat, how its intelligence and police forces managed the investigation and how its airport safety regulations did

or did not work. Twenty years later, these questions are still worth asking. The Air India bombings were the worst encounter with terrorism Canada has experienced. We cannot leave any issues unresolved.[2]

The Commission of Inquiry into the Investigation of the Bombing of Air India Flight 182 was established by Order in Council P.C. 2006-293, issued on May 1, 2006 pursuant to Part I of the *Inquiries Act*. (The Commission's Terms of Reference are reproduced in Annex A). The Commission was started on June 21, 2006 and continues to pursue outstanding issues relating to the tragedy. The passage of so many years made it difficult to obtain records and find witnesses. As a result the public testimony got off to a staggered start on September 25, 2006.

This first report seeks to identify the human element of Flight 182. From the disintegration of 329 lives only 131 bodies were recovered. Although the recovery of a body and the opportunity for proper burial brought a small degree of comfort to some families, sadly even that was denied to the majority, as 198 victims were swallowed by the sea. Entire families were lost, others were emotionally destroyed by the death of their loved ones, fracturing their home lives. The families and friends of the victims, as well as our society, have hope that this Inquiry will explain not so much what happened, but why it happened and how it can be prevented from happening again.

The bombing of Air India, coupled with the destruction of the World Trade Center's twin towers in New York City on September 11, 2001, created a heightened awareness of terrorism that has changed our society. Our level of comfort is fragile. Increased security measures, travel restrictions and general unease are now our frequent companions.

A question that lingers among the families and other Canadians is *If Air India Flight 182 had been an Air Canada flight with all fair-skinned Canadians, would the government response have been*

---

[2] *Lessons to be Learned*, Public Safety Canada, 2005, p.2.

different? There is no way to answer that. As a country, we would hope not. At the conclusion of the Inquiry, a better understanding of the events and actions that took place may help us all to decide.

The Commission heard most of the families' evidence between September 26 and November 17, 2006. (See Annex B for a list of witnesses). The persistent raw emotions of their experience, suffering and sorrow had to move the feelings of all who listened. Some accounts had been documented previously in books, articles and the media. In other cases, individuals who had earlier chosen not to speak came to be heard. What was different this time was that the families were invited by this Commission, mandated by the Government of Canada, to express their feelings in a formal public hearing before a government-appointed Commissioner. It is hoped the process of relating such personal grief will bring some healing to them. By speaking before the Commission, family witnesses have become the public conscience. By listening, the audience validates their experiences. Transcription in an official record makes their tragedy a part of our history. In this way, the further passage of time cannot erode the public memory of the enormity of what happened. The pain and loss it inflicted upon the families and communities of those who perished cannot be erased.

The majority of the people who bear this emotional burden are Canadians. Others are citizens of India, the United States, Ireland and the United Kingdom. Many of the rescuers in Ireland risked their lives in a frantic effort to keep the bodies from descending to the depths of the Atlantic Ocean. All of them expressed the hope that a public inquiry would help to prevent similar tragedies.

This report relates to events that took place before, during and after the Air India bombing. But its perspective differs from those in previous reports. Its purpose is not to chronicle history that is already well-documented, but to record the human toll that emerged from those events. It is understandable that the passage of time can be a deterrent to reliving such personal experiences in a public setting. For that reason, not everyone affected by the bombing gave evidence, some due to death and others because of a choice to remain silent. All living family members of the victims retain painful memories going back two decades. It is impressive that so many people maintained the will to testify and came forward after such a long time.

The transcripts of the hearings contain all the testimony from every witness. Both spoken and written words are recorded in the Commission's evidence. In addition, we have received printed, audio and video materials from many who testified and others who did not travel to Ottawa but wished to have their perspective heard. These materials form part of the Commission's official public record.

This report is based on the entirety of the evidence, evidence that is now public and available. The Commission's intent was to use examples from the evidence to portray the enormity of the destruction of Flight 182, its emotional effect, and the means adopted by families to cope. Our purpose is to record a composite of the human element, the resulting consequences of that June day 22 years ago.

This first report is being released before the Inquiry is complete because the families of the victims of the Air India tragedy have already waited much too long for their stories to be told. The publication of this report will mark the first opportunity for Canadians, and particularly young Canadians, to be able to fully understand the tragedy that befell many of their fellow citizens over 22 years ago.

These are not easy stories to read. The pages that follow are permeated with an ineffable sadness that is emotionally draining, but the examples of courage and determination that are related through the narratives illustrate the strength that accompanied the desolation of the victims' families.

A sense of grief was present throughout the hearings, but it was accompanied by guarded optimism and the resolve not to be defeated. There was the evidence of the families as well as the rescuers and others who attempted to alleviate the pain. It was *Mark Stagg* who captured the prevailing mood in these words:

> *But it is the families of Air India Flight 182 that take my breath away and of whom Canada should be so proud. They have a grace and dignity in the face of such suffering that has been both humbling and a source of renewal and restoration of my belief in humanity. My pain is dwarfed by that which these people have suffered without respite for 21 years and yet they still have the love to reach out to me and offer comfort. I never have to explain. They understand. And I say again, I am humbled.*[3]

J. C. Major
Commissioner

Monument at Ahakista, Ireland

1

---

[3] Mark Stagg, *supra*, September 27, 2006.

Outline

This document is organized as follows:

Section I (The Human Loss) tells stories about some of the victims of the bombing.

Section II (Heroic Efforts) and Section III (The Canadian Response) relate stories of people who were on the scene immediately after the crash and in the days following.

Section IV (The Aftermath) describes ongoing grief and ways in which memories of the victims have been preserved and honoured both personally and through public events and memorial sites.

Section V (Reconciliation and Hope) relates stories of individuals who organized and rallied family members to ensure that they never gave up hope in seeking justice and an inquiry to bring their emotions and concerns into a public forum. Section V concludes with actions taken by family members and friends in an attempt to deal with their own loss by helping others.

Throughout the report are graphical images including a selection of photos from those submitted by family members. These are numbered in sequence from 1 - 62. Captions for these images are listed in Annex D.

NOTES

- Every effort has been made to ensure the proper spelling of family names and place names. In some cases where there were variations, the Commission has consulted the families and other sources to select the preferred spelling.
- We have also consulted expert sources for the common spelling of foreign words.
- All quoted testimony appears in *italics*.
- The names of victims appear in ***bold italics***.
- The names of rescue/recovery workers are also in ***bold italics***.
- Where errors in spelling and punctuation occur in testimony, we have taken the liberty of making corrections.
- Some testimony has been condensed without losing the sense or intent of the original.
- Since these are the family stories there may appear to be some errors in fact or inconsistencies in certain testimony. The reader is cautioned to consider this to be the opinion of the witness (always cited in the footnotes) rather than the view of the Commission or any other party.
- Quotation marks are used for short descriptions, nicknames and quotes within referenced statements, e.g., *His mother cried out "help me" during the night*.
- Most of the photos reproduced in this report were submitted by family members. Commercial or other sources for photographs are acknowledged in the captions.

1
The Human Loss

Unfulfilled Potential

When listening to the painful recounting of events and the personal experiences and memories of family members of the victims of the bombing, it was immediately apparent that there was an enormous loss of human potential. Parents and children, scholars, scientists, doctors, social workers, business people, artists, humanitarians and students, perished as a result of that cowardly act of terrorism. Their disappearance created an emptiness within their families and where they worked, studied or volunteered. When they died, their many talents and skills, hopes and dreams went with them. In addition, the disaster affected the thousands of people they touched directly or indirectly through their work and community involvement.

Shakuntala, Uma, Sandhya and Swati Sharma

Shakuntala Sharma, a high school vice-principal in India, took her first vacation in 40 years in 1985 to visit her two daughters Usha and *Uma* and their families in Canada. She had been separated from her husband in 1947 when he became a political prisoner as a result of the partitioning of India and Pakistan. She never gave up hope of being reunited with her husband. *Shakuntala Sharma* had earned both bachelor's and master's degrees and raised her five daughters alone.

One of those daughters, *Uma Sharma*, an intelligent student who had earned her master's degree at the age of 20, finished first in her program and received the gold medal for outstanding achievement. She completed her Ph.D. in zoology and was an accomplished researcher. She worked part-time at McGill University in Montreal. Her husband Mahesh, also a Ph.D., was a professor of engineering at Concordia University in Montreal. On June 20, 1985, only two days before the tragic trip, the family gathered at a ceremony where Mahesh Sharma was honoured by the university with a Distinguished Teaching Award.

Uma and Mahesh Sharma's two daughters *Sandhya* and *Swati* were travelling to India with their mother and grandmother for a vacation in their parents' homeland. Both children were remarkably bright and accomplished even at their young ages. *Sandhya*, age 14, who tutored school friends to help them do better in class, was going to be surprised upon her

2-5

return home with the news that she had been named associate editor of the school paper, an assignment normally given to Grade 10 or 11 students. She was denied the opportunity to accept this honour. **Swati** was identified as a gifted student by her school board in Montreal. She was only 11, but already had plans to become an electrical engineer. The Protestant School Board of Greater Montreal had published two of her poems.

Shakuntala Sharma, **Uma Sharma**, **Sandhya** and **Swati Sharma** all perished on board Air India Flight 182. Four women spanning three generations from the same family were killed in a single attack.

Such a devastating loss has been difficult for the family, several of whom appeared before the Commission or submitted photos or written statements.[4] In one callous act, a massacre had wiped out three generations of accomplished and promising women. Their laughter would be heard no more, their potential snuffed out by the treachery of unseen assassins.

The Pain of Loss
By Smita Bailey[5]

Nobody can comprehend
The pain of loss I feel inside
So many years have passed
And I thought I would be stronger
Instead I remember, too clearly,
The laughter, the gentle voices, and the sparkling eyes…
I am forever wounded inside,
My heart forever broken
The crashing plane took all
And my soul remains shattered

---

[4] Mahesh Sharma, vol. 5, October 3, 2006; Smita Bailey, Mukta Laforte, Usha Sharma and Shridhar Sharma, all in vol. 7, October 5, 2006. In addition, three sisters living in India made written submissions: Asha Sharma (Exhibit P-57); Ila Sharma (Exhibit P-58); and Rama Sharma (Exhibit P-59).

[5] Vol. 7, October 5, 2006, p. 726, marked as Exhibit P-51.

Chandra and Manju Khandelwal

Chandra and *Manju Khandelwal* were born in India in 1964 and 1965 respectively. Their father, Dr. Ramji Khandelwal, came to Canada in 1968 to pursue his doctoral degree and was persuaded by his teachers and colleagues to remain here. The balance of his family joined him in 1973 during his post-doctoral studies at the University of California at Davis. They moved to Winnipeg in October 1975. The father became a Canadian citizen in 1980. The girls became Canadian citizens in 1983. Today, Dr. Khandelwal heads the Department of Biochemistry in the College of Medicine at the University of Saskatchewan. His primary research focus is on the use and impacts of insulin in the treatment of diabetes.[6]

Chandra and *Manju Khandelwal* were outstanding students who aspired to contribute to society through medicine. *Chandra*, a "very sociable" and affable young woman, was entering her third year of pharmacy at the University of Saskatchewan. As her father told the Commission, [s]*he chose pharmacy because she always believed that she wanted to have a good, balanced life between a professional life and a family life. She thought that as a pharmacist she can be full-time, part-time or whatever, and this way she can really balance her life very well between the professional and the personal family life.*[7]

6-7

---

[6] Testimony of Dr. Ramji Khandelwal, vol. 6, October 4, 2006, p. 648.
[7] Testimony of Dr. Ramji Khandelwal, vol. 6, October 4, 2006, p. 650.

Chandra was outstanding academically and a gifted flautist. She enjoyed cooking, sewing, knitting and activities with her younger sister. The girls were close.

Manju was less outgoing but equally loving and family-oriented. Like *Chandra*, she had musical talent and played the clarinet. While in high school, she told her parents of her interest in how plants and humans grew and functioned. She decided in Grade 10 to become a medical doctor and began to volunteer as a "candy striper" at a local hospital. *Manju* had a remarkable academic record. She completed high school in two years and pre-medicine in one and was admitted to the College of Medicine at the University of Saskatchewan at 18. At 19, the year of the bombing, she was about to enter her second year of medical school.

Their brother Deepak testified on the opening day of public hearings. He recounted that in June of 1985 he had decided to attend a summer computer course at the University of Calgary. He had a ticket for Air India Flight 182 but chose to skip the flight and accept a scholarship for the summer program.[8] Their mother, Vimla Khandelwal, had travelled ahead of the family and awaited the arrival of her daughters to celebrate the wedding of their father's younger brother in India.

> …I became an only child because of the bombing… I will never have the opportunity to attend my sisters' weddings. This thought haunts me at every single wedding I attend, as well as, I am sure, my parents.[9]

While travelling to their uncle's wedding on June 23, 1985, these two talented and promising young women were lost, leaving a devoted family behind.

> This preventable event destroyed my life as well as that of my parents. It took away from Canada and the world a future doctor and pharmacist who would have had tremendous positive impact on society, both personally and professionally.[10]

---

[8] Testimony of Deepak Khandelwal, vol. 1, September 25, 2006, p. 83.
[9] Testimony of Deepak Khandelwal, vol. 1, September 25, 2006, pp. 81-82.
[10] Testimony of Deepak Khandelwal, vol. 1, September 25, 2006, p. 81

Barsa Kelly

8

Barsa Kelly obtained a master's degree in geography in Florida after graduating from university in India. She then enrolled at the University of Toronto to pursue her Ph.D. **Barsa Kelly** met her future husband Kenneth Kelly in graduate school. They moved to Waterloo, Ontario and eventually to Guelph where both taught at the university. **Barsa Kelly** was completing field work for her doctorate at the time of her death. Her thesis dealt with rural women in West Bengal, India, and its completion would have improved their lot. She had temporarily postponed her doctoral work in order to devote attention to her two young daughters, Lorna and Nicola.

Her devotion went beyond her husband and children. She was a tireless and dedicated community worker and gave her time to many causes. Her daughter Lorna stated that her mother:

> *...was a dedicated volunteer and a strong contributor to her communities, locally and in India. In Canada, as a board member, she worked with the YMCA, Match, CIDA, Women in Crisis, IODE, and the Coalition of Visible Minority Women. Her involvement with the Coalition of Visible Minority Women was so valued that a new cooperative housing building in Toronto sponsored by the group was named in her honour posthumously. Organizations to which she contributed valued her humour, intellect and commitment.*[11]

[11] Submission of Lorna Kelly, vol. 4, September 28, 2006, p. 428.

Barsa Kelly was an educator and mentor to many women. She was an activist and feminist. She spoke out on important causes. The trauma of her death was too much to bear for her mother-in-law, who died from the emotional stress a few months after the mass murder. Lorna Kelly developed breast cancer five years after the bombing, with a second episode seven years later. Her oncologist attributes the onset of that illness to the extreme emotional trauma she endured from the killing of her mother, the process of identifying bodies and an ongoing feeling of responsibility for her family's emotional well-being.

Her sister Nicola Kelly presented a video submission to the Inquiry on October 10, 2006. In it, she described with sadness the lack of attention to the families of victims for so many years and offered a number of suggestions for strengthening the weak links in our system. She continues to mourn the sudden loss of *the best and most loving mother and wife.*[12]

---

[12] Video submission of Nicola Kelly, Exhibit P-64, October 10, 2006.

Dr. Anchanatt Alexander

Dr. Anchanatt (Mathew) Alexander immigrated to Canada in 1971 to begin post-graduate studies in surgery at the University of Alberta in Edmonton and brought his wife, Esmie, and their infant son, Robbie, to this new country. **"Alex"**, as his friends called him, specialized in cardiac surgery and completed his residency in general surgery at McMaster University in Hamilton, Ontario.

9

He was chief of staff at the West Haldimand Hospital in Hagersville, Ontario and maintained two general practice offices. Although he worked hard, he also ensured that weekends were spent with his family which had grown to three children by 1974.

Dr. Alexander was active in a variety of church and community causes and was admired by those whose lives he touched. This motivated and compassionate surgeon had forged a powerful life partnership with his wife:

> *I remember attending a talk about relationships between husbands and wives and realized that my husband had all the qualities of an ideal husband. He was understanding, supportive, loving, enjoyable to be around, and valued my opinion. He regularly used to consult me on issues that arose at the hospital. Though I don't know anything about medicine, he valued my judgment about people and he would use those opinions to make decisions he wasn't sure about.[13]*

---

[13] Submission of Esmie Alexander, vol. 4, September 28, 2006, p. 420.

Their son Rob recalls how after his father's death he had to quickly assume more responsibilities at home. His grandfather went to Ireland and was told that **Dr. Alexander's** body was not recovered, so a memorial service was held in July. Then, a call came in late October from the External Affairs department:

> *As the authorities were bringing up the wreckage from the ocean he was found attached to one of the seats of the plane… we got his body returned to us in early November… We then held a proper funeral for my father and had to go through the entire emotional trauma once again…*[14]

Dr. Anchanatt Alexander and his wife Esmie planned on moving back to India once the children were old enough to live alone in Canada, not because they did not love Canada, but to help less fortunate people who had little access to medical care. When **Dr. Alexander** boarded Air India Flight 182 to visit his ailing mother in India, that dream disappeared.

---

[14] Testimony of Robbie Mathew Alexander, vol. 5, October 3, 2006, p. 505.

Nagasundara, Jyothi and Thejus Radhakrishna

Nagasundara ("Nagu") Radhakrishna was travelling to India with her daughter *Jyothi* and son *Thejus*. Her husband Haran Radhakrishna, who remained behind, had completed doctoral studies at the University of Waterloo and was employed by Ontario Hydro's research division in Toronto after his graduation in 1967. He and *Nagu* married in 1969 and the children were born in 1971 (*Jyothi*) and 1977 (*Thejus*). *Nagu Radhakrishna*, considered "the focal point" in their family, was a sociable and friendly woman, active in volunteer work, particularly the children's school. She had earned a science degree in India, but had not yet entered the workforce, preferring to be with her children until they were grown.

10-11

Jyothi, 14, was described by her father as having a growing interest in humanitarian work. She wanted to help people in distress. She had attended her graduation ceremony from Grade 8 the night prior to the flight.

> *…she had some kind of a spiritual insight and she was a rare child indeed… She was a soft-spoken person and was very involved in her culture and religion. She was a pacifist and often intervened in the conflicts in her friends' circle.*[15]

Little *Thejus* was a bright, friendly and precocious child, apparently with few inhibitions. He was eight at the time he was murdered in the bombing.

---

[15] Testimony of Haranhalli Radhakrishna, vol. 9, October 11, 2006, p. 864.

I felt the emptiness when I returned to Toronto and came back to our home. I could not shake it off. My life had turned upside down. Some days after my work, I would drive to the ice hockey arena where my daughter used to go for practice, only to realize that she was not there anymore. My life was empty.[16]

A caring mother and two promising children were among the victims of the Air India bombing of June 23, 1985.

Peace Please

By Jyothi Radhakrishna

Let the time become ripe, let us wait
Let things become all right
Let there be no bloodshed or war
Let feelings of happiness prevail, not ones so sore
Let the answers be peace, let the fighting cease
Let us be together like the birds of the same feather
Let peace be won, let no one hold a gun
Then we shall live happily forever [17]

---

16 Testimony of Haranhalli Radhakrishna, vol. 9, October 11, 2006, p. 868.
17 Written in her school journal on June 7, 1985 only two weeks before her departure on Air India Flight 182, quoted in testimony of Haranhalli Radhakrishna, vol. 9, October 11, 2006, p. 865.

Syed Qutubuddin, Shaiesta, Rubina, Arishiya and Atif Quadri

Syed Qutubuddin ("Ather") Quadri had a successful career as a mechanical engineer with General Electric in Toronto. His wife **Shaiesta Quadri**, the first daughter in her family after four sons, was the apple of her parents' eye and lacked nothing. She had a good education and had a positive, jovial outlook on life. She left her family life in India to marry **Ather** and together they decided to settle in Canada. It was their chosen home.

Shaiesta Quadri's brother, Aleem Ehtesham Quraishi, came to Ottawa from Dubai to testify before the Commission on October 5, 2006:

> *My sister…loved life to the fullest. She felt that every day was a new day and that it was important for her to take time for the little things in life.*[18]

12-13

The Quadri family was close-knit. **Ather** was dedicated to his children's upbringing and the two girls responded by being top students:

> *Both daughters were extraordinary in their studies. Usually, children at that age are fond of TV programs, especially cartoons, but these kids were more into books and academic studies. Rubina was extraordinary in numerics and won many prizes in school.*[19]

Rubina Quadri was nine years old, and, as her uncle stated, already an accomplished student. At the age of four, her younger sister **Arishiya**

---

[18] Testimony of Aleem Ehtesham Quraishi, vol. 7, October 5, 2006, p. 667.
[19] Testimony of Aleem Ehtesham Quraishi, vol. 7, October 5, 2006, p. 668.

Quadri had demonstrated academic ability too. Whatever they might have accomplished or whatever they could have become was destroyed by the Air India bombing. Their baby brother **Atif Quadri** was 10 months old when the entire family was murdered. Of the five victims, four were never found. Only **Atif**'s body was recovered and taken to Hyderabad, India, for burial.

As was the case for other families, an inability to cope with the disaster led to further losses of family members:

> *The most affected one by this tragedy in my family was my father. He was, by nature, very sensitive and fragile, but very social and fun-loving as well. He was a retired civil servant, a very talented and well-known singer of his time. After the tragedy, though he kept himself away from friends, clubs and parties, he kept his talent until the last days and used to sing only in remembrance of my sister. He slowly deteriorated and died six years later...*[20]

---

[20] Testimony of Aleem Ehtesham Quraishi, vol. 7, October 5, 2006, pp. 671-672.

Sanjay and Deepak Turlapati

Sanjay and **Deepak Turlapati** were 14 and 11 years old respectively in 1985. Their mother, Dr. Padmini Turlapati, was in a paediatrics residency in Newfoundland. The boys lived in Toronto with their father Lakshminarayana "Babu" Turlapati, a chartered accountant. Born in India, the Turlapatis had worked in Nigeria for 10 years before immigrating to Canada in 1982. Their goal was to give their boys a broader perspective and greater opportunities in what they saw as their new and welcoming multicultural land.[21]

14

Their sons had demonstrated academic excellence and strong moral values. **Sanjay** was bright, alert and *mature beyond his years.*[22] He excelled in math, French, English and science. He wrote poetry which his teacher planned to collect in a book. He had received an award for top academic standing and had asked permission from his parents to take that award and many others, both academic and sports, to India when visiting grandparents and other family members.

Deepak *was also very bright, full of life and zest. He was a good negotiator, a good actor and determined. He too did well in school.*[23] He had negotiated his way into having a paper route at the age of 10 although the designated age for the job was at least 12. His compassion was evident through the kindness he showed an elderly woman on his paper route. On one unseasonable day, he checked to see whether she needed anything and was asked if he would

---

[21] Testimony of Dr. Padmini Turlapati, vol. 2, September 26, 2006, p. 188.
[22] Testimony of Dr. Padmini Turlapati, vol. 2, September 26, 2006, p. 189.
[23] Testimony of Dr. Padmini Turlapati, vol. 2, September 26, 2006, p. 189.

go buy her milk. **Deepak** gladly did so and received a two dollar tip for his efforts. At home, when he showed his tip to his father, Babu Turlapati chastised him for accepting money after doing a favour for an older person. The young boy returned to the lady's home and said he could not take her money. This lady later called Dr. Padmini Turlapati to say she had wept for **Deepak** as if he were her own son.

Only a day before his flight, **Deepak** told his mother that he had a premonition of his death and asked her to save him. On the day of the flight, he remained behind in the house to say goodbye to each piece of furniture in his room, which left his mother "aghast."

Dr. Padmini Turlapati travelled to Cork, Ireland to identify the bodies of her children:

> I picked out a face with an expression of pain that turned out to be Sanjay's body. He is the only one of all the victims who was fully clothed, missing only a Hush Puppy shoe as if to say "Mom, believe I am here."[24]

Deepak's body was never found. **Sanjay's** body was taken to Vijayawada in India, where both sets of grandparents lived:

> We buried Sanjay and a picture of the Atlantic Ocean water to represent Deepak there.[25]

---

[24] Testimony of Dr. Padmini Turlapati, vol. 2, September 26, 2006, p. 193.
[25] Testimony of Dr. Padmini Turlapati, vol. 2, September 26, 2006, p. 194.

Muktha and Deepak Bhat

Muktha Bhat came to Canada following her university graduation. She was sponsored by her brother who lived in Toronto. She met and married Krishna Bhat while visiting India. In 1974 they settled in Ontario, where her husband worked as a petroleum engineer. In 1983 the family moved to Sherwood Park, Alberta where Krishna Bhat joined a team starting a new oil refinery.

Krishna Bhat earned sufficient income to enable his wife to leave her job with Canada Post and stay at home with the children. Both parents had previously worked on different shifts, with little time left for family activities. The move to Alberta corrected that.

15-16

> *We had a happy home. She was active in the community, involved in the church and enjoyed singing. She was a very talented classical singer. She was also good at knitting and making her own dresses.*[26]

Deepak Bhat was nine years old in June 1985. Described by his father as "very talented" and a good piano player, *Deepak* was also athletic and enjoyed participating in track and field activities at school. He wanted to become a doctor and help people.[27]

The family trip to India had been scheduled for July 6th, but a niece had called to convince

---

[26] Statement of Krishna Bhat, vol. 5, October 3, 2006, p. 528.

[27] Exhibit P-303, *Love, Honour, Respect: The memories of our loved ones* developed by Mona Sandhu and Smita Bailey, produced through the Family Members of the Victims of Air India Flight 182 and Narita, British Columbia Ministry of the Attorney General, 2005, p. 46.

Muktha Bhat to come earlier and visit. Prior to the June 22nd flight, **Deepak** feared for his safety. He wanted to delay the trip to India in order to participate in track and field activities at his school. His father assured him that everything would be fine.

Krishna Bhat told the Commission that after hearing news of the disaster, a strange feeling of being in a void and helpless prevailed around him. **Deepak's** body was never recovered. Krishna Bhat is critical of the treatment of family members by Canadian officials and continues to mourn what might have been:

> *Perhaps he* [former prime minister Brian Mulroney] *never thought that it happened in our own backyard. Alas, what a twist of irony. Are we not Canadians? Were not those talented children, including a dear Deepak, the future of Canada?*[28]

---

[28] Statement of Krishna Bhat, vol. 5, October 3, 2006, p. 536.

Broken Dreams

Among the victims were individuals and families embarking on new experiences in their lives – a marriage, a new business venture, new educational opportunities, travel adventures.

There were young children who had been studying a new language in order to enrol in school in India. There were world travellers who sought to learn about the rich culture and history of India and its people. There were business people who had achieved success in Canada and sought opportunities for investment in India.

Their hopes and dreams came to an end with the destruction of Air India Flight 182. Individuals, families and friends were thrown into chaos by the death of their loved ones. The grief creates a space that cannot be filled. This broken bond is irreplaceable. Fleeting memories often haunt those who are left.

Vinubhai, Chandrabala, Bina and Tina Bhatt

Vinubhai Bhatt, his wife *Chandrabala*, and their daughters *Bina* and *Tina* were on their way to India *to set up a business in India and live happily after with the whole family.*[29] *Vinu Bhatt*, who travelled abroad to obtain an MBA following a law degree in his native India, had come to Canada with his wife and daughter *Bina* in the early 1970s. Their second child, *Tina*, was born in Canada and all four were Canadian citizens.

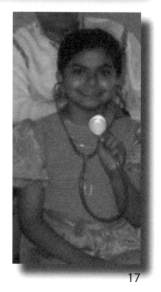

17

Vinu Bhatt had been working with a cup manufacturing company in Toronto as the general manager, but had planned to establish a business in India where there was a large extended family. In addition, his daughters had studied Hindi and were eager to study in India and learn more about their heritage.

The family was happy in Canada. Their nephew Laxmansinh Abda spoke before the Commission and described *Vinu Bhatt* as "hardworking" and *Chandrabala Bhatt* as "an ideal housewife". The daughters were both brilliant children in school. *Bina* was intent on becoming an astronaut; *Tina* wanted to become a doctor and help children in need.[30]

The family was extremely close. *Vinu had seven days planned. He never neglected the family. Every day they had planned...they never separated.*[31] They had strong values. The girls always brought Donna Ramah Paul small gifts to express their love and affection and she found

---

[29] Testimony of Laxmansinh Abda, vol. 10, October 12, 2006, p. 992.
[30] Testimony of Laxmansinh Abda, vol. 10, October 12, 2006, p. 991.
[31] Testimony of Donna Ramah Paul, vol. 8, October 10, 2006, p. 789.

them to be unusually caring and affectionate children. They were urged to look their best as they journeyed to meet family in India. The parents wore their finest clothing and jewellery, as though they were a bride and groom. When Donna Ramah Paul made the painful trip to Cork, Ireland, three bodies were identified: *Both the children looked like angels as if they were sleeping, the same clothes they were wearing.*[32] **Vinubhai Bhatt's** body was not found.[33]

---

[32] Testimony of Donna Ramah Paul, vol. 8, October 10, 2006, p. 806.
[33] Testimony of Laxmansinh Abda, vol. 10, October 12, 2006, p. 993.

Rachelle Castonguay

Rachelle Castonguay grew up in St. Isidore de Prescott near Ottawa. She attended the University of Ottawa and earned her master's degree in geography in 1981. She was a social researcher and had completed work for the Mackenzie Valley Pipeline Hearings in 1975-76. In addition, she had prepared various papers on northern socioeconomic concerns for the Northern Science program within the Department of Indian and Northern Affairs. At the time of her murder, she was employed in that department as a policy analyst. Her understanding of northern issues and northern peoples was deep. She was a valued member of the department's northern science team.

18

Rachelle Castonguay was a champion of many causes, including famine relief in Africa, women's rights and the promotion of the French language in Ontario.[34] She was also a devotee of nature. She explored parks, toured by bicycle, went camping and took photographs of the wonders around her. She loved to travel and discover new places, people and cultures. Her trip to India was intended in part to provide material for her forthcoming Ph.D. dissertation.

On June 23, 1985, her dreams ended and the nightmare began for surviving family members. **Rachelle Castonguay's** body was never recovered.

Her family, like so many others, has sought answers since the bombing and encountered the same frustration and disappointments:

---

[34] *Love, Honour, Respect: The memories of our loved ones*, p. 62.

But exactly what government help could have assisted us, and on the other hand, what help from the government was actually available? There was no such help and nobody made a big deal out of it. All of us were extremely shaken by this turn of events and left to our own devices. [35]

---

[35] Testimony of Monique Montpetit-Castonguay (translated), vol. 5, October 3, 2006, p. 454.

Dara D. Dumasia

Dara D. Dumasia was a veteran of 31 years with Air India and was the flight engineer on Flight 182. Sadly, he was four months from retirement. He was survived by his wife Sheroo and his daughters Dilshad and Farnaaz.

Sheroo Dumasia declared in a written statement to the Commission:

> *Our lives were shattered. We were absolutely inconsolable in our grief.*[36]

As the only wage earner in the family, **Dara Dumasia's** death left his widow and family vulnerable economically and distraught emotionally.

> *Lack of security was immense both financially and emotionally. Death is always unacceptable to those left behind to grieve but in this instance it was the unexpectedness of it, the senselessness of the disaster, that was so appalling.*[37]

Dara Dumasia had over 14,000 hours as a flight engineer.[38] He was due to retire on October 30, 1985. His death denied him his well-earned retirement.

---

[36] Submission of Sheroo Dumasia, vol. 11, October 13, 2006, p. 1023.
[37] Submission of Sheroo Dumasia, vol. 11, October 13, 2006, pp. 1023-1024.
[38] *Love, Honour, Respect: The memories of our loved ones*, p. 84.

Krishnakumar Gopalan

A few days before the flight, **Krishnakumar ("Kishan") Gopalan** graduated from Carleton University in Ottawa with a degree in mechanical engineering. He was 23 years old. His sister, Dr. Chandra Vaidyanathan, is a paediatrician practising in Ottawa. Their late father was also a medical doctor. She appeared before the Commission as did her brother Ramachandra, a chemical engineer in India.[39]

19

Kishan Gopalan had been a gold medalist at the Coimbatore Institute of Technology in India, where he earned an engineering degree. He moved to Canada to pursue another engineering degree at Carleton University and graduated with distinction. He was returning to India to visit prior to beginning work as a mechanical engineer with Pratt and Whitney Canada. He died never having had a chance to commence his employment. Dr. Chandra Vaidyanathan described her brother as a mechanical genius who fixed everyone's television, radio or phone line.[40]

He became the master of the house, providing all necessary love, affection and assistance to my parents. He became so close to them that my father even thought that there was nothing in this world that Kishan does not know. Fixing even small things for him, right up to cleaning up his car, backing it up, keeping it ready for him to leave for the clinic, so many things my father and mother depended on him every day.[41]

39 Testimony of Dr. Chandra Vaidyanathan vol. 6, October 4, 2006, p. 579 and testimony of Ramachandra Gopalan, vol. 8, October 10, 2006, p. 814.
40 Testimony of Dr. Chandra Vaidyanathan vol. 6, October 4, 2006, p. 581.
41 Submission and testimony of Ramachandra Gopalan, vol. 8, October 10, 2006, p. 819.

Many dreams were left unfulfilled with **Kishan Gopalan's** sudden death. A promising career in aerospace was abruptly terminated. His brother, relying on major input from **Krishnakumar**, was forced to scale down construction plans for a new home. His mother, proud of her son's academic and athletic accomplishments, had planned to return to Canada to be near him and to continue teaching dance, drama, singing and music. She withdrew instantly and permanently from all activities and public appearances following the death of her youngest son.

> *My mother, more than anyone in the family, has suffered the most with incalculable proportion, the loss of her sweet boy. She had dreams of building a life after losing her husband with the strength of her young son and watching him attain greater heights in life. But after she heard the news of this great tragedy, she went into dark depths of despair, never to recover even to today. She is under constant medication to keep her nerves. She becomes hysterical at times and becomes reclusive avoiding all social activity which was a part of her vibrant lifestyle before losing him. We were never able to pull her out of this tragedy.*[42]

20

---

[42] Testimony of Dr. Chandra Vaidyanathan vol. 6, October 4, 2006, p. 584.

Satwinder Singh Bhinder

Satwinder Singh Bhinder was co-pilot on *Kanishka*. He had been both a commercial and a military pilot (he fought in two wars in 1965 and 1971). At the time of his death, his greatest pleasure was being with his family – his wife Amarjit, his daughter Jasleen and his son Ashamdip. Had it not been for the beginning of the children's school year in India, his wife Amarjit would have been on board Air India Flight 182.

21

> *He loved his small world which had his wife and two children.*[43]

> *…I was very lucky to have him as my husband. He was a great son, a loyal and caring husband and a doting father, and above everything else a great human being.* [44]

Undoubtedly, **Satwinder Bhinder's** life as a pilot had a major influence on his children. Ashamdip would often wear his father's uniform shirt – he is now a pilot with Indian Airlines. Jasleen is married to a pilot with Singapore Airlines.

Amarjit Bhinder told the Commission that after the crash they became penniless, although she received some funds from the Indian Pilots Guild. There was no compensation from the Canadian government, and, as with other crew members who do not purchase tickets, there was no flight insurance.

---

[43] Submission and testimony of Amarjit Bhinder, vol. 11, October 13, 2006, p. 1005.
[44] Submission and testimony of Amarjit Bhinder, vol. 11, October 13, 2006, p. 1003.

I lost control over myself. My children heard my cries and they too started howling. I can never forget their faces.[45]

She could not send her daughter to England after high school as had been hoped, and both children's school grades dropped for several years after their father's death.

Every June 23rd, the family offers prayers in Gurudwara[46] Sahib. As Amarjit Bhinder reflected on the senselessness of the bombing in her written statement to the Inquiry:

What did we do to deserve a life with a void that will never be filled?[47]

To magnify the effects of the tragedy, her husband's body and those of the other crew members were never found:

Destiny cut short the life of a brilliant pilot and a person whose vision was unparalleled in Air India and whose intelligence rare to find.[48]

[45] Submission and testimony of Amarjit Bhinder, vol. 11, October 13, 2006, p. 1007.
[46] A Sikh place of worship (or temple) – the name means "doorway to the Guru".
[47] Submission and testimony of Amarjit Bhinder, vol. 11, October 13, 2006, p. 1013.
[48] Submission and testimony of Amarjit Bhinder, vol. 11, October 13, 2006, p. 1004.

Gaston Beauchesne

Gaston Beauchesne was a seasoned traveller, a man of the world, "a bon vivant". The Trois Rivières native was a pharmacist by profession. As a business venture, *Gaston Beauchesne* toured extensively and arranged travel packages for pharmacists to distant places such as China, Japan, and Egypt. In fact, he was on his way to Egypt via India when he booked a flight on Air India 182.

22

Gaston Beauchesne's death cut short his renewed relationship with his son Eric and his daughter Dianne. As Eric Beauchesne told the Commission:

> My parents divorced when I was little…As my sister and I grew older we began to reconnect. I think that my father dealt with us better as grownups than as children.[49]

Eric Beauchesne was fortunate enough to see his father just before his flight. They had lunch and coffee and *Gaston Beauchesne* let Eric drive his Trans Am sports car which 20-year-old Eric thought to be "kind of cool". About that last day with his father, Eric Beauchesne recalled:

> …And the part that really stands out about that day was that I was able to hold him, hug him, and tell him I loved him and say goodbye, and he was able to tell me he loved me before he said goodbye and left. And it's a memory that I really treasure because I'm sure there's a lot of people who didn't have that chance and it's something that I really hold on to.[50]

49 Testimony of Eric Beauchesne, vol. 6, October 4, 2006, p. 631.
50 Testimony of Eric Beauchesne, vol. 6, October 4, 2006, p. 632.

Dianne Beauchesne's last memories of her father were in stark contrast. In Ireland to identify his body, she saw the photo of her father and recalled how frightened he looked:

> ... the sheer terror on his face was just unbelievable.[51]

As she told the Commission in her videotaped submission, her father wanted to start a business with her and Eric, in yet another attempt to bring them closer as a family.

Eric and Dianne Beauchesne were troubled by the lack of support from the Canadian government. Adding to the lack of recognition and response was the fact that when Dianne Beauchesne arrived in Ireland, nobody treated her as a family victim because she was Caucasian:

> We didn't have the appearance of what everybody thought the Air India meant. But Air India was a Canadian terrorist tragedy.[52]

Eric Beauchesne spoke of the "invisible tragedy" to Canadians, because he felt the Canadian government treated it as something remote, something that happened far away on a non-Canadian airline, unrelated to Canada.

Still lacking closure on her father's death, Dianne Beauchesne asked a question that holds true for all the victims:

> How can you put a value on someone's soul, on someone's life, on their expectations, on their dreams, on their hopes, their wishes?[53]

---

[51] "How Do You Say Goodbye to a Loved One?", video submission of Dianne Beauchesne, vol. 12, November 6, 2006, p. 1098.

[52] Video submission of Dianne Beauchesne, vol. 12, November 6, 2006, p. 1098.

[53] Video submission of Dianne Beauchesne, vol. 12, November 6, 2006, p. 1113.

Indira Kalsi was 21 years old in June of 1985. Her parents and brother Raj had already gone to India, but she stayed behind to complete a college course. She was enrolled in nursing studies at the University of Guelph and had earlier completed a college diploma as a nursing assistant. She worked part-time almost daily as a pharmacy assistant and expressed the hope that she would one day dispense free medication to underprivileged people in India.

Indira Kalsi's part-time job in Mississauga, Ontario, was a significant distance from her university in Guelph, but she never complained. That was her character. She was a selfless, devoted and caring daughter and sister. Her father, Rattan Singh Kalsi, told the Commission of her generosity in buying him a car from her part-time earnings. Her kindness in giving time and gifts extended beyond her family. *Indira Kalsi* visited senior citizens' residences in her home town. She also helped older people who lived on their own. *Indira Kalsi* cleaned their houses, brought them flowers, and arranged for cakes on their birthdays. As a result of these generous acts she often arrived home late, to the consternation of her parents.[54]

Indira Kalsi's, cousin, Surjit Kalsi, said that as was common in their community, he considered her a sister and said that *it hurts too much to talk about Indira and the tragedy.* [55]

This remarkable young woman boarded Air India Flight 182 to attend her brother's wedding. Her violent death understandably ripped a hole in the hearts of the family and the community she left behind.

> *Parents should die in an old age in front of their children, not the children …in front of the parents…Somebody killed our children.*[56]

---

[54] Testimony of Rattan Singh Kalsi, vol. 9, October 11, 2006, p. 879.
[55] Submission of Surjit Kalsi, Exhibit P-50, vol. 7, October 5, 2006, p. 708.
[56] Testimony of Rattan Singh Kalsi, vol. 9, October 11, 2006, p. 872.

Meghana Sabharwal

Meghana Sabharwal was 12 years old. She lived in Bombay, India[57] with her mother and brother, but her father Promode Sabharwal was based in London, England, at that time. She had spent three months in Montreal visiting her grandmother and other family members in Canada and planned to return home on Flight 182.

Meghana's father described her as a *very brilliant student* whose ambition was to teach and to be a leader in that field.[58] He remembers her as an outgoing child with many friends, and a young girl with *a lot of general knowledge*.[59]

Promode Sabharwal went with his brother to Cork, but was unable to find **Meghana**'s body. He returned to London and then to Bombay to join the remaining family. He told the Commission that he found the memories of **Meghana**'s childhood and her growing up in Bombay to be too painful. He could not bear to be in that environment and decided after a few months to move to Montreal to stay with his brother.

After two years, he became a landed immigrant and then brought his family over to Canada. Collectively, they had to separate themselves from the painful memories of Bombay:

> *...and then I had my family come after two years...And we had to start again...*[60]

---

[57] The official name of the city changed to Mumbai in 1995.
[58] Testimony of Promode Sabharwal, vol. 6, October 4, 2006, p. 573.
[59] Testimony of Promode Sabharwal, vol. 6, October 4, 2006, p. 573.
[60] Testimony of Promode Sabharwal, vol. 6, October 4, 2006, p. 575.

Lakshmi and Veena Subramanian

Lakshmi Subramanian and her daughter **Veena** were to visit her mother in India. Her husband, Murthy, had declined to go because he was planning a family trip to Disneyworld in Florida.

23

Lakshmi Subramanian had joined her husband in Canada in 1972. In 1975, their first child was born, but tragically died within two days. Later that year, **Veena** was born.

Veena was a special child. Her aunt, Jagada Venkateswaran, remembered the straight-A student as being *very intelligent and warm*.[61] Murthy Subramanian emphasized how his daughter *had many friends in our family circle and in school*.[62] In fact, her school teacher, Ms. Palmer, remembered **Veena** in a condolence card as a kind, humble and modest girl and someone who:

> ...shared all of her things with everyone. She worked hard at school, helped other children with their work, had a lovely smile, was a peaceful child, a little princess at school.[63]

Lakshmi Subramanian, the wife and mother, was described as a beautiful, loving, caring person. In his written statement to the Commission, Murthy Subramanian stated that on identifying her body in Ireland:

---

[61] Statement of Jagada Venkateswaran, vol. 2, September 26, 2006, p. 236.
[62] Submission of Murthy Subramanian, vol. 4, September 28, 2006, p. 413.
[63] Submission of Murthy Subramanian, vol. 4, September 28, 2006, p. 413.

I was terribly shocked to see her pretty face was so damaged due to the impact of falling towards the ocean from a 33,000-foot altitude.[64]

Prior to leaving London for Cork to identify her body, he had been troubled by the apparent absence at the Heathrow Airport of Canadian government officials or professionals to deal with grief.[65]

In contrast, Air India had arranged for free passage to Ireland from Canada and once there *the Indian Ambassador was very helpful and supportive.*[66]

Although he had no contact from Canadian officials, Murthy Subramanian did receive a letter of condolence from then-prime minister Brian Mulroney.

At work, his employer was highly supportive of him. The company provided him with six months of leave with pay and an additional three months on June 23, 1986.

Murthy Subramanian established scholarships in India and Canada to commemorate the lives of his wife and daughter. Every year he travels to Bangalore, India, where his wife is buried. The body of **Veena Subramanian**, *a beautiful little girl,*[67] was never found.

---

[64] Submission of Murthy Subramanian, vol. 4, September 28, 2006, p. 416.
[65] Submission of Murthy Subramanian, vol. 4, September 28, 2006, p. 415.
[66] Submission of Murthy Subramanian, vol. 4, September 28, 2006, p. 415.
[67] Submission of Murthy Subramanian, vol. 4, September 28, 2006, p. 413.

Ardeshir K. Enayati

Ardeshir K. Enayati was a retired marine engineer who immigrated to Canada with his wife Freny and two younger children (Zeeba and Shahin) around 1980 to live near their three children already in Canada (Farida, Firdaush and Rukhshana).[68] The Enayatis had chosen to retire to Canada rather than one of the many other countries they had seen while travelling.

Not content to stay idle in retirement, **Ardeshir Enayati** began work as a professor of marine engineering in Montreal. At the time of his death, he was on leave from his position as a professor at André Laurendeau CÉGEP (a junior college) in Lasalle, Quebec, a Montreal suburb.

Ardeshir Enayati practised the Baha'i faith, and in his retirement taught classes on it. He was the only Baha'i member on the flight. His widow stated to the Commission:

> *The Baha'i religion was formed in 1863…We believe men and women are both alike. They each have full rights. We believe in all religions, Hindu, Muslim, Sikh, Catholic, Christian, Zoroastrian, etcetera.*[69]

This distinguished scholar, humanist and world traveller was on his way to India to sell his property and settle accounts so that his retirement in Canada would be complete.

Ironically, one of **Ardeshir Enayati**'s bags had to be taken off the plane at Mirabel Airport because it had triggered a false security alert. His grieving widow said: *I often wish he had also been pulled from the flight, not just his bag.*[70] As fate would have it, the confiscated bag was all that Freny Enayati would retain from that flight. Her husband's body was never found.

---

[68] Family names are taken from *Love, Honour, Respect: The memories of our loved ones*, p.85
[69] Submission of Freny Enayati, vol. 11, October 13, 2006, p. 1029.
[70] Submission of Freny Enayati, vol. 11, October 13, 2006, p. 1031.

In the aftermath, like so many others, her quiet, comfortable life took a dramatic change:

> *All my life I had taken care of my family, never had a paying job. After my husband died, I took a nanny's course for three months because I needed money to live. I worked as a nanny.*[71]

Instead of enjoying her retirement years, she had to start over, guided by her Baha'i faith and bolstered by fond memories of her devoted husband.

---

[71] Submission of Freny Enayati, vol. 11, October 13, 2006, p. 1031.

Great Leaders, High Achievers and Role Models

Among the victims of the bombing were many planning or in the midst of meaningful careers; others had begun to enjoy their retirement. These individuals were leaders in various fields including, but not restricted to, medicine, science and education. Their achievements are exemplary, first to the families who survived them and to our society. Their contributions to Canada and the world remain as a permanent record of what they accomplished during their abbreviated lives.

Many of the victims were the strength and beacons in their extended families. They had assumed the roles of family providers, caregivers, guidance counsellors and taken on many responsibilities. As a source of support, strength and guidance, they would be greatly missed by those who depended upon them.

Dr. Sugra Sadiq

Dr. Sugra Sadiq was born into an Iranian family that immigrated in the 1920s to the south Indian city of Hyderabad. During the Second World War, she volunteered as a nurse. Her son Ali Tahir recalled:

> In these desperate times people were fleeing out of their responsibilities, ignoring cultural traditions, abandoning manners, selling children and relatives, basically grabbing anything just to survive, but not our mother, even though she was in a minority and fragile community.[72]

Sugra Sadiq was one of the first female students in medical school. She demonstrated excellence and achieved top grades in all her years of study. **Dr. Sadiq** encouraged her husband Syed to pursue his studies and he too succeeded and became the principal of a teachers training college. **Dr. Sadiq** specialized in maternity and fertility work and helped many couples to have children both in India and later in Canada. Her son said that her knowledge was valued by colleagues:

> …she was always an anchor in the circle of the medical profession. Doctors of all sciences, homeopathic, allopathic or holistic; everyone recognized her dignity and respected her. In family and social community, she was a pastor, a model, a counsellor.[73]

Throughout her studies and medical career, she continued to have and raise her children, 10 in all. Three moved to North America to live in what they thought to be a safer and more peaceful environment. Inspired by their parents' work ethic and success, the children pursued careers in medicine, dentistry, public service, accounting, education and industry.

After retirement and the death of a son in a train accident, the Sadiqs moved to Toronto to enjoy their later years in the company of their

---

[72] Submission of Ali Tahir Sadiq, vol. 11, October 13, 2006, p. 1015.
[73] Submission of Ali Tahir Sadiq, vol. 11, October 13, 2006, pp. 1015-1016.

children. Her husband taught, translated technical articles and lectured. **Dr. Sugra Sadiq** periodically gave medical advice and found comfort in teaching principles of Islam at Sunday school, and Persian, her mother tongue, to students at the University of Toronto.[74]

To **Dr. Sugra Sadiq**, family, education and service to society were all-important. Just two days before Flight 182, she attended the convocation ceremony during which her youngest son graduated from York University in Toronto.

> *She was a woman ahead of the times, an anchor for her large family and many friends. Those she left behind were left helpless without her.*[75]

---

[74] Dr. Sadiq spoke English, Persian, Urdu and Telugu: *Love, Honour, Respect: The memories of our loved ones*, p. 263.
[75] Submission of Ali Tahir Sadiq, vol. 11, October 13, 2006, p. 1017.

Dr. Nayudamma Yelevarthy

Dr. Nayudamma Yelevarthy[76] was an internationally renowned scientist, government advisor and academic. He had been a science advisor to the cabinet in India. He studied industrial chemistry at Banaras Hindu University and took advanced studies in both the U.K. and U.S. He was a major catalyst for developing the Indian leather industry and a strong proponent of national economic development using enhanced knowledge and technological innovation in the leather sector. He was an early supporter of India's Central Leather Research Institute (CLRI) and became its director in 1958. Under his stewardship, the CLRI flourished, becoming the largest institute of its kind in the world.

Dr. Yelevarthy was active as a professor at the University of Madras, with Indian and international students. His specialized knowledge in leather technology was known worldwide. He served on the boards of many public and private-sector organizations. He was a governor of the International Development Research Centre (IDRC) in Canada as well as an advisor to the United Nations. His credentials in scientific research, government advisory work and scientific publications were extensive.[77] His credo was that science existed to better the lot of people and that research and education must have the ultimate goal of improving opportunities and living conditions.

This scientist, educator, humanist and visionary was killed on June 23, 1985. He was returning to India from an IDRC governors' meeting in Canada.

The shock of his sudden death was too much for his wife, Pavana, who was a medical doctor. She attempted suicide when she heard of the bombing. Their eldest son, Ratheish Yelevarthy, was left to deal with a double tragedy. He flew to Cork to retrieve his father's body. But his body was not recovered. After a short time in Cork, where he stressed that the efforts of the Irish were *a touch of milk of human kindness*

---

[76] In the literature, his name often appears as Yelevarthy (or Yelavarthy) Nayudamma. The family name "Yelevarthy" has been confirmed and that is the form used in this report.
[77] More biographical highlights of Dr. Nayudamma Yelevarthy's career and accomplishments can be found in *Love, Honour, Respect: The memories of our loved ones*, pp. 215-218.

that poured[78], he returned to India and learned that his mother had succumbed to her suicide attempt. Funeral services were conducted for both parents at the same time. The intensity of his personal sorrow expanded exponentially when Ratheish Yelevarthy, after the memorial rituals for his parents, learned that his young son had accidentally drowned in a pool. Soon after, his grandmother died from the shock. His ability to recover and to go on with his life is a marvel which is inspirational.

It is difficult to understand such human suffering, precipitated by the random murder of a world-renowned scientist whose mission was to help people live better lives. All that remains is the anguish of those left behind.

> *Life has never been the same after my father's death for all the family members and some of his grandchildren never got to see him. He would have given us high moral support and indirectly it was a name for all of us to refer to, to be proud to, be related to. He was a man liked by everybody and he meant so much for so many of them. On the news of his death, we received condolences from people in many parts of the world.*[79]

---

[78] Statement of Ratheish Yelevarthy, vol. 11, October 13, 2006, p. 1037.

[79] Submission of Ratheish Yelevarthy, vol. 11, October 13, 2006, pp. 1038-1039.

Drs. Zebunnisa and Umar Jethwa

Mohammad Irfan Umar Jethwa was orphaned by the Air India bombing. His mother **Dr. Zebunnisa Jethwa** and father **Dr. Umar Jethwa** were physicians. **Umar** was 45 and **Zebunnisa** was 43 when they died on June 23, 1985. They were accomplished surgeons and had completed their resolve in 1980 of founding a hospital in Ankleshwar, India.

24

The **Jethwas** were tireless workers who treated all in need of medical care. Where they lived poverty was prevalent, and much of their work was charitable. **Dr. Zebunnisa Jethwa**, a skilled gynaecologist, was widely sought by Muslim women who preferred not to be treated by male doctors.

All was for serving mankind in a better way. They never had a commercial aspect of their private practice in their minds. I still remember… they wanted to serve mankind and money would come naturally. Serving mankind was better than anything else they always taught me. Service to mankind is service to God… They used to treat poor and needy people free of charge and even pay for their medicines. Still poor and needy people remember them with a tear in their eye. Ankleshwar was not a big town at that time and had many poor and needy people in and around.[80]

---

[80] Submission of Mohammad Irfan Jethwa, vol. 8, October 10, 2006, p. 838.

Irfan Jethwa, their son, now 33, works in India as a computer network engineer. **Dr. Umar Jethwa**, his father, had founded a school and had with him at death a personal computer for the pupils to use. He had written to Irfan about this from Vancouver while on vacation. Ironically, they decided on the June 22nd Air India flight, one that was earlier than they had planned, because they were anxious to be reunited with their young son. Irfan's aunt, Banu Saklikar,[81] and cousin, Renee Saklikar, both told the Commission how this terrorist attack had shattered their family. The loss of these gifted and caring physicians has been a loss not only to the family and to India but, by their example, a loss to all of us. It is inspiring how their young son, in the words of his cousin Renee Saklikar, managed to recover from this loss and grief to rebuild his life:

> Irfan grew up alone. I do not know how he did it, but he has survived. He is a kind, intelligent entrepreneurial self-contained man, a family man, with a loving wife and two sons of his own.[82]

---

[81] Written statement of Mrs. Banu Saklikar, vol. 7, October 5, 2006, Exhibit P-48.
[82] Testimony of Renee Saklikar, vol. 7, October 5, 2006, p. 694.

Captain Narendra Singh Hanse

Narendra Singh Hanse was the captain of Air India Flight 182. He was, after 35 years of flying, close to retirement and planned to return home to rural India. He was among the airline's most experienced pilots, and an active participant in the Indian Pilots Guild, where he served as both general secretary and president.

25

While active in the Pilots Guild, he had improved working conditions (and "perks" as his widow noted).[83] He devoted time to making the Guild a strong organization from its humble beginnings.

His son Anil, a trained deep sea diver, had been with **Captain Hanse** in Toronto on the day of the flight, but left to take an earlier flight to London en route to Aberdeen for a diving assignment in the North Sea. Anil Hanse often had radio contact when his father was in flight. His sudden death devastated Anil. He postponed his diving career because of the loss:

> I was trained as a deep sea diver, but found I was unable to continue with this career after my father's death. Much of this was due to the memories and close relationship I had with my father. When I was at sea, Dad would radio the oil rig I was working on and pass messages to me. He would wish me well and confirm our upcoming meetings. This would give my workmates an opportunity to rib me and every plane in the sky was cause for this ribbing to begin anew, and it took me years to return to the diving industry.[84]

83 Testimony of Sheila Singh Hanse, vol. 10, October 12, 2006, p. 964.
84 Testimony of Anil Singh Hanse, vol. 10, October 12, 2006, p. 969.

Anil Hanse married two years after his father's death. His wife, Swaran Singh Hanse, noted that although she never met **Captain Hanse**, she and her children are very much aware of the difficult circumstances under which he perished and that the children wept with her and Anil at the acquittals. She told the Commission that:

> The sense of frustration and helplessness has on many occasions seeped into our life, saddening us considerably. My mother-in-law, who lives in a granny flat near us, has failing health and we know that she grieves constantly for the lack of her life companion.[85]

---

[85] Statement of Swaran Singh Hanse, Exhibit P-79, vol. 10, October 12, 2006, p. 966.

Sam Madon

Sam Madon was born in Bombay and navigated the world's oceans. He had completed his captain's exams successfully in South Shields, England and sailed with different shipping companies for years. He married his childhood sweetheart, Perviz, and they travelled to Iran and England and eventually migrated to eastern Canada in the early 1970s. Shortly thereafter, they moved west to enjoy milder winters.[86] Their children Eddie and Natasha were born in Vancouver, British Columbia.

26

Sam Madon loved his work, but it was second to his family. He did not want to be away for prolonged periods and looked for a job at home. In 1978, he was hired to teach at Marine College in North Vancouver and became a respected instructor. He published two books on navigational aids. Natasha Madon attended the Commission's hearings with her mother and recalled incidents about her father's teaching career. One was about a former student she met by accident who recognized her name and told her how her father had been instrumental in changing his life. *Sam Madon* had seen him struggling in class and insisted that he stay late after school for private lessons:

> And I guess my dad was quite relentless that he got it and spent every evening with him until he did and he always remembered him for it.[87]

---

[86] Testimony of Perviz Madon, vol. 6, October 4, 2006, p. 590.
[87] Testimony of Natasha Madon, vol. 6, October 4, 2006, p. 592.

Another involved a student who could not afford tuition fees. **Sam Madon** gave him private tutoring without charge and was proud when he became a navigational officer.[88]

He was remembered as a devoted husband and a caring father. He insisted that his wife not work in order to raise the family. His spare time was spent with the children:

> He made sure that he was involved in their everyday lives… it was a hard job to teach and come home tired but he would be the soccer coach for Ed's team. He would take them to the park. He adored Natasha. We enrolled into ballet when she was three-and-a-half, just prior to his death, and at her very first ballet concert, he just was such a proud father. He must have taken I don't know how many photographs of Natasha in her little tutu and her ballet tights and he would incessantly talk about that to all our friends, how proud he was of his children. [89]

In early June of 1985 **Sam Madon** stayed behind to complete his teaching duties while the rest of the family went to visit in India. He took the later Air India Flight 182 to join them.

In spite of the shock and profound sadness that followed the sudden death of her husband and so many others, Perviz Madon told the Commission that she counted herself to be luckier than others:

> I was one of the so-called lucky ones to have found his body, because apparently from the 329 only 131 bodies were recovered, and out of that 131 bodies recovered there were only 13 male bodies, the rest were children and women. So I was extremely blessed to at least have him back and put him to rest with dignity and have a kind of a closure with that.[90]

---

88 Testimony of Natasha Madon, vol. 6, October 4, 2006, p. 592.
89 Testimony of Perviz Madon, vol. 6, October 4, 2006, p. 593.
90 Testimony of Perviz Madon, vol. 6, October 4, 2006, pp. 596-597.

Bhagwanti Gogia

Bhagwanti Gogia, a recent widow, immigrated to Canada in 1983 to live with her son Ram.[91] She had been a pillar of support in her family. As Ram Gogia told the Commission: *She had four children all of whom she took care of with love.*[92]

27

After Ram Gogia's younger brother died tragically in an accident, his mother helped look after his family, including assisting her son's widow in running a plastic parts manufacturing business.

Her planned trip to India on Air India Flight 182 was, as could be expected, all about family:

> *My mother was very excited about her trip to India. It was going to be a very busy trip as she had many family members to take care of.* [93]

Her death in the bombing of the aircraft created a huge vacuum in the family. Her daughter-in-law in India had to close her business, as she could not continue with work and family without **Bhagwanti Gogia**'s assistance.

Every year, Ram Gogia attends a memorial at Dow's Lake in Ottawa, joining members of other victims' families to reflect on their loved ones and all the lives they had touched.

---

91 Mrs. Gogia's name appears in *Love, Honour, Respect: The memories of our loved ones*, p. 95.
92 Statement of Ram Gogia, vol. 11, October 13, 2006, p. 1026.
93 Statement of Ram Gogia, vol. 11, October 13, 2006, p. 1026.

Mohan Kachroo

Mohan Rani Kachroo ("**Nana**") came to Canada in the 1970s from Kashmir. Her daughter Vijay Kachru told the Commission that **Nana Kachroo** came from a very traditional Brahman family, *where women were supposed to be seen – actually, a lot of times not even seen and not heard definitely.*[94]

28

In Saskatoon, **Nana Kachroo** found new freedom. She no longer felt bound by norms of dress and behaviour. She learned to speak English and was intent on obtaining a driver's licence. She opened a daycare centre, became a businesswoman, as well as a Canadian citizen:

> *She said she was Canadian. She didn't even say she was Indian-Canadian. Hyphenation was not important. She was just Canadian.*[95]

Her granddaughter, Meera Kachroo, appeared before the Commission and read a statement from her parents Romesh (**Nana Kachroo**'s son) and Irene. It told of how **Nana Kachroo** was the person who held the family together when times were tough. They wrote with pride that:

> *She taught by her example, prayer, calmness, fairness, gentleness, customs and rituals. Her thinking was all-inclusive. She was in Canada only for seven years, very full years, as a contributing resident.*[96]

---

[94] Testimony of Vijay Kachru, vol. 7, October 5, 2006, p. 759.
[95] Testimony of Vijay Kachru, vol. 7, October 5, 2006, p. 769.
[96] Submission of Romesh and Irene Kachroo (Exhibit P-61), read by Meera Kachroo, vol. 7, October 5, 2006, p. 777.

The results of her example were impressive. By age 21, Vijay, her daughter, had already obtained two master's degrees. Romesh Kachroo, her elder son, obtained a master's in mathematics and the younger son, Balkrishan, had a master's in linguistics.

Vijay Kachru told the Commission of her last day with her mother:

> We had breakfast somewhere…we went shopping at Ogilvy's in Montreal…we went to a little coffee shop and ordered french fries and tea with ketchup.[97]

Nana Kachroo, now totally emancipated, was on her way to India to celebrate her 60th birthday and to *show off to her brothers, brothers' wives, everybody else, how much she had changed, became her own woman*.[98] She felt safe boarding Air India 182, safer than if she had been in Srinagar in her native Kashmir, where she would have needed armed guards to protect her from insurgents.[99]

Her mother's death was particularly hard on Vijay Kachru:

> I used to be able to talk to the presidents of corporations, just look them in the eye and talk, be a Canadian, be a woman… After this, for the longest time, I couldn't do it.[100]

She told the Commission how her younger brother renounced Canada, his Canadian citizenship and his Canadian passport. In fact, she feels that somehow they belong to an "underclass" by being associated with the Air India matter:

---

[97] Testimony of Vijay Kachru, vol. 7, October 5, 2006, pp. 764-765.
[98] Testimony of Vijay Kachru, vol. 7, October 5, 2006, p. 759.
[99] Testimony of Vijay Kachru, vol. 7, October 5, 2006, p. 766.
[100] Testimony of Vijay Kachru, vol. 7, October 5, 2006, p. 768.

> *The community as a whole has been broad-brushed with you're not worth it, move on, this happens, there are wars, just move on.*[101]

How difficult this would have been for **Nana Kachroo** to accept – she, a true Canadian. As her daughter said, *she and the victims were not citizens of convenience.*[102]

Nana Kachroo's husband, Nagindra Mohan Kachroo, wrote a book of poems dedicated to her memory. His granddaughter, Meera, read one of these poems to the Commission:[103]

A Past Reflection
By Nagindra Mohan Kachroo

*I remember the day when I saw you for the first time
as an image reflected through a glass mirror.
That moment is etched in my mind as an
eternal seal, an image of an indelible nature
printed on the mirror of my consciousness,
not everlasting, since that would be in the field of time,
but eternal beyond time.
I do not remember the descent, but I do remember
when we met flying on the wings of time.
A great time it was indeed in a mortal way, and then
you flew away.*

---

[101] Testimony of Vijay Kachru, vol. 7, October 5, 2006, p. 771.
[102] Testimony of Vijay Kachru, vol. 7, October 5, 2006, p. 773.
[103] Read by Meera Kachroo, vol. 7, October 5, 2006, p. 780.

Om Prakash Sharma

Om Prakash Sharma married Krishna when he was 16 and she 14, but their official married life commenced only when his wife was 16. Their devotion was constant and, with her support, he completed his studies and became the principal of a middle school in India:

29

> *Our family was not rich by any standard but my husband was a very hardworking individual and he always encouraged me, inspired me and supported me.*[104]

The Sharmas had eight children and eventually **Om Prakash Sharma** found it difficult to support his family on his salary as a principal. He was a voracious reader and inspired his siblings and children to take their studies seriously. As the eldest son, he felt it was his responsibility to care for his aging parents, so they too lived in his home, as did his widowed sisters. This was all made possible with the support of his wife. In 1972, he moved to Canada to increase his income.

> *Being the eldest in the family he was responsible to take care of my aunts and uncles, financially, emotionally, and morally. He was a role model to them. He wanted to give us and his brothers and sisters better lives, so he applied for a job in Canada and Australia. He got accepted for a teaching job in Middle Arm, Newfoundland. He was a high school principal when he left India to provide a better life to his children, parents, and wife.*[105]

---

[104] Statement of Mrs. Krishna Sharma (translated from original in Hindi), vol. 10, October 12, 2006, p. 936.
[105] Testimony of Veena Sharma, vol. 10, October 12, 2006, p. 954.

For 14 years, **Om Prakash Sharma** worked and saved to improve the welfare of his family in India. Each summer he would return home to share two months with them. Several of his children so missed their father that they followed him to Canada. His daughter Saroj spoke to the Commission of her father's hobbies:

> He loved wrestling. He was an ayurvedic[106] doctor. He used to make herbal medicine and give free to his community people. Because of… these hobbies people would call him stuntman or sometimes herbal doctor.[107]

Om Prakash Sharma always hoped that the family would be reunited in Canada. Before Flight 182, he told his wife that this was his last trip to India and that he intended for her to return to Newfoundland with him. The children, some of whom were already with their father in Canada, were happy at the prospect.

Several family members who spoke to the Commission reflected about having premonitions of danger prior to his flight, and stated that they told their father to cancel the trip. He dismissed their worries.

The explosion ended his dreams and hopes, opening wounds that have yet to heal. His daughter, Neelam Kaushik, told the Commission that she has progressively lost faith in the government, police, intelligence services, airport security and now the justice system. She recalled how difficult it was for her to cope, to smile or even to be civil. She was angry most of the time and shouted at those close to her. She said that the frustration has split her family:

> The anger and frustration my family felt at the system for not producing anything constructive regarding the case, we took that anger out on each other. So the family that was once very close drifted apart to the point that we don't even talk to each other anymore, and that's very disheartening for my mother.[108]

---

106 Ayurveda is a form of holistic alternative medicine traditionally practised in India. The name derives from the Sanskrit words for "life" and "knowledge".
107 Written Statement by Saroj Gaur, vol. 10, October 12, 2006, p. 940.
108 Testimony of Neelam Kaushik, vol. 10, October 12, 2006, p. 945.

Another daughter, Madhu Gaur, sent a written statement to the Commission. She was saddened by her perception of shortcomings in the Canadian criminal system and described the family suffering resulting from her father's unnecessary death.

> …our family lost its head, its unity. Losing a parent is a great loss indeed that cannot be fulfilled. We found support from friends and family elders. However, we did not ever find justice from the Canadian justice system.[109]

---

[109] Written Statement of Madhu Gaur, vol. 10, October 12, 2006, p. 961.

II
HEROIC EFFORTS

Responding to the Emergency

In the midst of sorrow and confusion, some people are able to raise the human spirit and perform deeds of bravery and kindness. This happened when Air India 182 exploded off the coast of Ireland. A number of individuals quickly dedicated themselves to the treacherous challenge of finding survivors in the wreckage; and when that proved unsuccessful, they accepted the grim task of helping with the effort to recover the victims and their belongings. Others on shore opened their homes to the families in need. Such was their generosity that the families were first surprised, then overwhelmed, by the Irish kindness and many remain as friends with frequent contact.

Seanie Murphy

Seanie Murphy lives on Valentia Island (also spelled Valencia) off the southwest coast of Ireland. He has worked since 1982 for the Royal National Lifeboat Institution, a non-government agency that seeks to preserve life at sea throughout the British Isles. Virtually everyone on his island is involved in some capacity with the lifeboat operation:

30

> ...this was an Arun class lifeboat. It's 52 feet in length. It's a 17-foot beam. It's a 5.5- foot draught. It's got two 500-horsepower Caterpillar engines and...she has a top speed of 18 knots... And she burns 50 gallons an hour.[110]

A pager system is now used, but in 1985 when an emergency arose the crew was called into action by rockets fired from the Arun. After earning his skipper's ticket in England, **Seanie Murphy** was invited to become captain of his lifeboat in 1981. His crew included a full-time engineer and volunteers from different parts of Ireland.

He had gone to mass on the Sunday morning of June 23rd and met a man who told him that a marine radio station had advised that a plane had gone off the radar screen in Shannon. After the church service, **Seanie Murphy** learned that this was a disaster. He mobilized his crew and set sail, knowing that they were venturing *110 miles* out into the ocean, more than double their usual range. He knew that going twice as far into the waters than was the norm would severely strain the fuel supply.

When **Seanie Murphy** testified at the Commission, he wanted to remember the people who accompanied him on that mission. Most were volunteers with no training for events like the Air India bombing.[111] These men were:

---

[110] Testimony of Seanie Murphy, vol. 3, September 27, 2006, pp. 269-270.
[111] Testimony of Seanie Murphy, vol. 3, September 27, 2006, p. 270.

Joseph Houlihan, engineer, age 47;
Richard Connelly, fisherman, age 32;
James Murphy, fisherman, age 40;
Eamonn Murphy, car mechanic, age 25;
Shane O'Neill, fisherman, age 24;
Nealie Lyne, property manager, age 30; and
Seamus Murphy, student, age 17

The trip to the scene of the crash took almost seven hours. When **Seanie Murphy** realized that he had no charts to cover the disaster area, he took another chart and *I turned it upside down as a blank sheet of paper and I extended the lines of latitude and longitude onto it and I used this as a dead reckoning system to plot the course out to where we were going.*[112]

Although they were accustomed to recovering people in distress or the dead from accidents at sea, they were ill-prepared for what they encountered:

> *We had recovered bodies from the sea before. That's our line of work, but never to the scale of this. We never expected this.*[113]

Once in the area of the crash, they spotted debris and suitcases. As they moved closer to the main search area, bodies were seen. In about two hours, they recovered four bodies and then, about to leave and return to shore, one crewman spotted the body of a young child. The crew recovered it and barely spoke about that recovery during the long trip home. **Seanie Murphy** paused to collect himself while testifying as he recalled how he then thought of his own three-month-old daughter. He told the Commission of a strange pervasive silence, even among the crew and the citizens at the pier who had volunteered their help. In total, the journey had taken over 20 hours.

To this day, **Seanie Murphy** and his crew rarely discuss that recovery effort. He has met some of the families and has had to overcome a personal fear of flying stemming from the Air India crash. He told the

---

[112] Testimony of Seanie Murphy, vol. 3, September 27, 2006, pp. 271-272.
[113] Testimony of Seanie Murphy, vol. 3, September 27, 2006, p. 274.

Commission of the sad memories that return whenever he meets family members:

> …*when I meet them … it all comes back again…I see the suffering they're going through. But I just hope they get some peace somewhere along the way.*[114]

Mark Stagg was a 26-year-old third officer on the *Laurentian Forest*, a 23,000-tonne vessel making its way from Canada to London via Dublin carrying a cargo of newsprint. He was one of 26 British officers and crew aboard the ship. An urgent message came from Valentia radio at 8:44 a.m. on June 23, 1985 that an aircraft had disappeared from the radar. His first thought was that he and his crew could be *heroes to the rescue.*[115] By 9:44 a.m., the broadcast signal was upgraded to an SOS, with details of an Air India jumbo jet going down with more than 320 passengers.

31

Mark Stagg told the Commission that his captain, ***Roddy McDougall***, bravely ignoring fuel concerns, diverted the ship towards the crash area. Otherwise they would have been *37 miles* away and travelling in the opposite direction.

Even though the catastrophic nature of the accident was evident from the wreckage strewn across the crash site, for some time the crew remained hopeful of finding survivors. Perhaps it was their inherent unwillingness to admit that their efforts might be in vain.

Although there was no indication of survivors as they came to the crash area, ***Mark Stagg*** remained cautiously hopeful. When he saw bodies floating in *a sea covered with a sheen of aircraft fuel*[116], he began to grasp the enormity of the disaster. His earlier sense of adventure had disappeared:

> *I felt shock and dismay. This was out of the mental script that I'd written for myself. This was no longer a game. There was no play involved. I felt sick. I was scared, but we had a job to do and we will save some people and some of this will be okay.*[117]

---

[115] Testimony of Mark Stagg, vol. 3, September 27, 2006, p. 331.
[116] Testimony of Mark Stagg, vol. 3, September 27, 2006, p. 333.
[117] Testimony of Mark Stagg, vol. 3, September 27, 2006, p. 334.

A lifeboat was dispatched and with the aid of helicopters bodies were recovered. **Mark Stagg**, as previously noted, recalled for the Commission that he felt the boy in him had died that day when handed the corpse of a perfect and beautiful baby.

Mark Stagg said that his merchant vessel and crew were not equipped or prepared to deal with a plane crash. They had a useless stretcher and no body bags. Consequently, it was necessary to improvise using the semi-transparent nylon liners of inflatable dunnage bags. He felt that this makeshift option violated the privacy and dignity of the victims, but under the circumstances it was the best that could be done.

Mark Stagg lost his inner peace as a result of the recovery mission. The horror continues to revisit him in dreams and daytime flashbacks. In addition, he told the Commission that the colleagues with whom he served also continue to suffer from problems related to the crash. He will always carry with him the regret that not one person was saved:

> *I recall spending parts of the day keeping a tight rein on my feelings to the point of complete detachment and dispersed with periods of extreme grief, extreme anger, and almost hysterical laughter… I refused to discuss the event with anyone and as a result, suffered nightmares, flashbacks and periods of deep depression.*[118]

Some time after the recovery mission, **Mark Stagg** heard of post-traumatic stress syndrome and at his own expense sought medical help and counselling. In June 2001, when the RCMP contacted him about the British Columbia trials, his nightmares and flashbacks returned:

> *For brief instances of time I am transported back to that scene. It is real. I smell the smell. I see the things. I hear, I taste and feel all the stimuli. I am not there but I am there.*[119]

---

[118] Testimony of Mark Stagg, vol. 3, September 27, 2006, p. 343.
[119] Testimony of Mark Stagg, vol. 3, September 27, 2006, p. 345.

Mark Stagg gained the strength to attend the 2005 memorial service at Ahakista in Ireland. At the airport, he met his former shipmate **Daniel Brown** for the first time since the crash. They did not discuss their feelings and have since become friends. He also met Dr. Padmini Turlapati, who thanked him for recovering the body of her son **Sanjay**. As **Mark Stagg** stated, his heart broke. He is humbled by the actions of the family members who in the face of such loss still reach out to him with gratitude:

> *It was over for them before it began for us, but it is my everlasting regret that we saved no one, and yet she thanks me.*[120]

---

[120] Testimony of Mark Stagg, vol. 3, September 27, 2006, p. 347.

Daniel Brown

When **Daniel Brown** appeared before the Commission, he had been in the British Merchant Navy for 28 years. On June 23, 1985, he was a young man from Scotland making his second voyage on the *Laurentian Forest*. He was on watch duty when called up to the bridge, where he steered the ship beside his

32

captain, who was immersed in reports about the increasing severity of the crash.

The *Laurentian Forest* was the only merchant ship in the area that launched a lifeboat. **Daniel Brown**, a member of that crew, was asked to look for bodies. Of seven bodies recovered under adverse conditions, he helped with six. Many of the bodies were badly damaged and oil from the wreckage in the water made them difficult to grasp. **Daniel Brown** did whatever he could to recover bodies and load them aboard the lifeboat. Suddenly, he heard the second mate shouting. He realized they were in trouble as they were coming perilously close to the *Laurentian Forest*:

> ...*as we came under the stern, I had to go over and lie on top of the bodies to keep my head below the gunwale. The boat continued to come under the stern and the first time it hit, it was quite light really, but as we kept coming under the stern, we had more and more increasing impact and I thought the boat was going to break up.*[121]

The weight of the bodies on board the lifeboat greatly hampered its manoeuvrability and it came close to being crushed under the ship's stern. Only the ingenuity of the ship's captain saved them. **Captain Roddy McDougall** somehow managed to align his large ship with the lifeboat.

---

[121] Testimony of Daniel Brown, vol. 3, September 27, 2006, p. 299.

The next major problem was how to upload the bodies onto the ship. That too did not happen without compounding difficulties. Some crew were becoming ill and others were crying at the carnage. At one point, **Mark Stagg** shouted frantically. **Daniel Brown** then saw a body trapped in the propeller, and he wanted to get it free but he was forced to let it go. The challenges continued to mount. Even when the recovered bodies were finally transferred to the *Laurentian Forest*, they still had to be moved several times for various reasons.

After their return to Dublin, where they gave a statement to the local police, at the captain's suggestion they went for a drink. At the pub, while watching the arrival of the victims' families on the television news, **Daniel Brown** suddenly felt the impact and his emotions overtook him:

> *I just went back to the ship and I went in my cabin and just cried.* [122]

> *I went home on leave. I was having trouble sleeping. I was home for five weeks. Now, I've left that company. I'd already decided to leave it before this event, and I joined another ship. I was having a lot of trouble sleeping, sleep nightmares and flashbacks. I became aggressive and cynical, angry.* [123]

One of **Daniel Brown**'s shipmates never returned to sea and another never flew again. None of them were nor could they have been prepared for the horror and magnitude of the tragedy. **Daniel Brown** told the Commission that he suffered from post-traumatic stress syndrome for more than 10 years. His first treatment was sleeping pills. He was advised to seek counselling following the British Columbia trials. He developed better mechanisms for coping and has had an easier time dealing with the events of June 1985. He told the Commission of his feelings regarding the gratitude by the families of the victims, many of whom he has befriended:

---

[122] Testimony of Daniel Brown, vol. 3, September 27, 2006, p. 309.
[123] Testimony of Daniel Brown, vol. 3, September 27, 2006, p. 310.

The thing that strikes me most is the attitude of the people that lost more than anything else in this event. They're the ones that showed more gratitude. They thanked us for our efforts. They were thinking about us, as we were thinking of them. We all became friends with many of them.[124]

Daniel Brown told the Commission that his strong physical conditioning likely enabled him to delay the emotional impact for two days, but the enormity of what happened had a profound impact on him, as it did on his colleague **Mark Stagg**. Both of them continue to feel remorse at not having found even a single survivor:

I wish we could have got more. I wish we could have brought them all home, but I think the ocean beat us.[125]

---

[124] Testimony of Daniel Brown, vol. 3, September 27, 2006, p. 314.
[125] Testimony of Daniel Brown, vol. 3, September 27, 2006, p. 314.

Captain Roddy McDougall

Roddy McDougall was master of the *Laurentian Forest*. **Captain McDougall** died before the Commission's hearings began. He was acknowledged by his crew to be a skilled seaman and a strong leader. Decisions he made on June 23, 1985, contributed directly to his crew's ability to retrieve some bodies. **Daniel Brown** credits him with taking the lifeboat next to the *Laurentian Forest* out of danger:

33

> *...and although the second mate was making all the right manoeuvres, there was no steerage. Captain MacDougall was aware of this and ...he put the ship alongside the lifeboat which was quite a feat of seamanship.*[126]

His former officer and good friend **Mark Stagg** recalled for the Commission that **Roddy McDougall** was in failing health when evidence was being gathered for the British Columbia criminal trials, and he was unable to appear:

> *I talked to Roddy McDougall. He cannot give evidence. He has had a stroke and he is not a well man. We talk a lot and exchange e-mails. I arrange that in 2005 we will go to Ireland and maybe lay our ghosts.*[127]

Roddy McDougall wrote a letter to his corporate headquarters on July 1, 1985 to chronicle the events of June 23rd. It was published in the company's in-house journal[128] and introduced as evidence before the Commission.[129]

Roddy McDougall noted that every member of his crew volunteered in the effort to recover the bodies. They all dismissed a report that sharks had been sighted in the area and commenced their dives without hesitation. He called it "a long, sad Sunday" and paid tribute to his men:

---

[126] Testimony of Daniel Brown, vol. 3, September 27, 2006. p. 300.
[127] Testimony of Mark Stagg, vol. 3, September 27, 2006. p. 344.
[128] Harrisons (Clyde) Ltd., Glasgow, letter no. 22-85.
[129] Exhibit P-18, vol. 3, September 27, 2006, p. 354.

The Air India disaster only brings out the emotional feeling we all have at what we see. I do, however, have the satisfaction of knowing what an excellent crew I have.[130]

The Commission was given a letter written by the late **Roddy McDougall** to **Mark Stagg**. In it, he reassured **Mark Stagg** that he was not alone in his strong emotional reaction and shared some of his private horrors:

That day comes back every time I get settled on a plane. Also when I have restless nights and dreams of ships, the bodies in the water always get into the dreams and in particular, one Indian in blue denim shirt and trousers staring up at me… I will never forget him and some of the other awful sights of that day.[131]

The in-house journal's editor wrote a postscript to **Roddy McDougall**'s letter:

The operation carried out by the crew of Laurentian Forest on Sunday 23rd June required courage, endurance and skill. These qualities were found in great abundance. Everyone worked together unselfishly. Because of sea and weather conditions, none of the other merchant ships in the area launched a boat. The great sadness is that there were no survivors. But no praise can be too high for the men who continue to search and to pick up bodies despite physical and emotional strain for twelve hours. It was an heroic effort.[132]

---

[130] Capt. McDougall's letter, Exhibit P-18, reproduced in vol. 3, September 27, 2006, p. 358.

[131] Excerpt from a letter from Roddy McDougall to Mark Stagg, Exhibit P-19, reproduced in vol. 3, September 27, 2006, p. 359.

[132] Exhibit P-18, signed "IVRH", reproduced in vol. 3, September 27, 2006, pp. 358-359.

Mark Tait

Sergeant Mark Tait was a skilled diver in the Royal Air Force. He was on board a Sea King helicopter sent to retrieve bodies on June 23, 1985. Like other would-be rescuers, his original guarded hope was to save lives. That hope vanished upon encountering the grim scene at the crash site. His first retrieval was a doll. He was upset with himself that people might be drowning while he recovered a toy.

34

While his initial objective was to locate survivors, it became clear that the job was to recover victims. What **Mark Tait** found under the water has troubled him since 1985:

> *It was pretty bad and there was a lot of body tissue, fat, and I saw various body parts. I also swallowed a fair amount of sea water that had lumps in it. I must presume this was human flesh tissue or whatever. I don't know and I don't want to.*[133]

Mark Tait had to grab damaged and lifeless bodies from the water. He retains the image of an older lady wearing a sari whose body was literally split in two and too damaged to retrieve from the water. He cannot forget what he considers a personal failure:

> *Although I wanted to recover her body for her relatives…this was impossible, so I reluctantly watched her float away…quite a haunting image and a decision that still unsettles me.*[134]

Mark Tait told the Commission that he carries guilt about not returning that day to the crash scene after the helicopter returned to shore. He knew at that time that he would not be able to cope. Returning to the site the following day, no additional bodies were found. Later, when approached to give evidence, the memories overcame him and he had to seek treatment for clinical depression.

---

[133] Submission of Mark Tait, Exhibit P-17, vol. 3, September 27, 2006, p. 322.
[134] Submission of Mark Tait, Exhibit P-17, vol. 3, September 27, 2006, p. 323.

Initially, he was off work for nine months. Eventually, he was able to recover and become functional with the help of a psychiatrist in the RAF. **Mark Tait** retired from the RAF in 2004 and now works in the rail industry. In some way, he too was a victim of the terrorists.

He made a decision to attend the British Columbia trials and said that he does not regret doing so:

> The relatives were bound to be emotional, perhaps critical or hostile to our actions. I think going was the best decision we could have made. It was truly humbling, however uplifting, to meet the relatives. They were so kind and appreciative, not just of our actions but to our feelings as well. It was difficult to make small talk.[135]

Mark Tait remembers one encounter that he found to be personally invaluable. He spoke with an elderly lady who told him that the body of her daughter, a promising doctor, was not found:

> I said how sorry and guilty I felt that more bodies had not been recovered and she said that she preferred to remember her daughter as she was rather than have the pain of seeing her broken.[136]

Mark Tait recalls that he felt relieved and is grateful to that woman who does not know how much she helped him.

---

[135] Submission of Mark Tait, Exhibit P-17,vol. 3, September 27, 2006, p. 326.
[136] Submission of Mark Tait, Exhibit P-17,vol. 3, September 27, 2006, p. 326.

Thomas Hayes is a superintendent in the national police force of Ireland – *An Garda Siochana*. In Gaelic that means "guardians of the peace." He commands one of four districts in Cork City. He told the Commission of the force's mission "to achieve the highest attainable standards of personal protection, community commitment and state security"[137], which includes acting:

35

> ...*on behalf of the coroner in relation to deceased persons and we take a lead role in any major incident, with particular emphasis on investigating any criminal matter involved in such incident, public safety and recovery and identification of victims.*[138]

On June 23, 1985, **Thomas Hayes** was an entry level officer with the national police force and was attached to the station in which the Cork Regional Hospital was located. That hospital has subsequently become the University Hospital.

Thomas Hayes told the Commission of the extensive search and rescue force mobilized when the Marine Rescue Coordination Centre at Shannon received notification of the missing aircraft at 8:13 a.m. local time. The search force included ships from the Irish Navy, the Royal National Lifeboat Institution, the Royal Navy, the Royal Air Force, the United States Air Force and commercial vessels in the area. At 10:02 a.m., the *Laurentian Forest* was the first ship to arrive at the scene. The Irish naval vessel *L.E. Aisling* arrived at 11:45 that morning and played a coordinating role for the 18 ships participating in the search.[139]

---

[137] Testimony of Thomas Hayes, vol. 3, September 27, 2006, p. 361.
[138] Testimony of Thomas Hayes, vol. 3, September 27, 2006, pp. 361-362.
[139] Testimony of Thomas Hayes, vol. 3, September 27, 2006, p. 365.

Once the national police received notification of the disaster, the Major Emergency Plan for Cork City was activated. As **Thomas Hayes** recalled, the magnitude of the disaster was beyond anything they had experienced previously:

> *While this plan had been engaged, we did not at that particular point have a full sense of ... the full extent of the tragedy that we were facing. This was the first time that we in the Garda Siochana had to deal with a disaster of this scope.[140]*

Thomas Hayes was dispatched to the regional hospital to await the arrival of casualties, still unaware if there were any survivors. He correctly suspected the worst. He was assigned to work with a doctor and nurse in receiving bodies and recording their identifying characteristics. He described the overall process and the roles of the police officers, the meticulous measures taken to confirm identities and, once a match had been confirmed, the process of releasing the bodies to bereaved family members. He told the Commission that members of his force were compassionate, making *every effort to support the families in this difficult ordeal.* [141]

Between June 24th and June 27th, post-mortems were conducted with a team of seven pathologists and *each pathologist had a team consisting of a Garda ballistics expert, a Garda fingerprint expert and a Garda photographer.*[142] The process of identifying the bodies did not end until August 7, 1985. He also appeared as a witness at a coroner's inquest on September 17, 1985.

Thomas Hayes told the Commission that he recalled someone from the Canadian High Commission in London being on the scene from the first day, and that that person dealt with the Garda and the coroner. The High Commission official processed and facilitated the transfer of information during the investigation. He also acknowledged excellent cooperation from the RCMP, particularly in obtaining fingerprint records in Canada and in following up inquiries that came from the investigation team in Cork.

---

[140] Testimony of Thomas Hayes, vol. 3, September 27, 2006, p. 366.
[141] Testimony of Thomas Hayes, vol. 3, September 27, 2006, p. 374.
[142] Testimony of Thomas Hayes, vol. 3, September 27, 2006, p. 375.

Thomas Hayes reflected on the efforts of the Garda and many other agencies to work in harmony throughout the emergency:

> *What I remember about the time is the enormity of the task and the way everyone worked together to achieve a common purpose. The obvious goodwill and positive relationships formed between all agencies involved, and in particular with the families, left a very positive image. We were dedicated to identifying each of the individuals recovered and return them to their families. We succeeded in identifying all 131 bodies. We knew how important it would be to families to have their loved ones returned to them so that they could grieve properly and ensure that the families were given the opportunity to observe any religious customs.*[143]

---

[143] Testimony of Thomas Hayes, vol. 3, September 27, 2006, p. 380.

Gratitude for the Acts of Kindness in Cork, Ireland

Juxtaposed against the feelings of abandonment by the Canadian and the Indian governments were overwhelming expressions of gratitude for the generosity, outpouring of concern, selfless behaviour and love from the citizens of Cork, Ireland. Person after person told the Commission about the kindness of the Irish people. Virtually very family representative who came before the Commission had praise for the local agencies, priests, nuns, social workers, hospital staff, taxi drivers, hotel staff and general citizenry. The understanding, generosity and compassion of the people of Cork continues to be a source of strength and inspiration to the people whose families perished in the Air India bombing. For many, those human bonds forged in the midst of tragedy and loss remain strong. The friendships that emerged have endured and family members who return for memorial services continue to be treated with warmth, respect and a sense of belonging.

Other people, including the Indian High Commissioner and his wife, were cited by family members for their humanity in the immediate aftermath of the bombing.

The Kindness of the Irish

Throughout the first phase of the Inquiry, witness after witness commented on the kindness and generosity of the people of Cork, Ireland, and its surrounding communities.

Lata Pada told the Commission:

> The Irish…are indeed the world's most beautiful people, most compassionate, most caring. They took this tragedy upon themselves as if they had suffered and they had and they demonstrated such an incredible sense of kinship, such an incredible sense of humanity and compassion.[144]

Not only did the frontline emergency responders devote themselves to the tasks of dealing with the horror, but ordinary citizens rose to the occasion. Zerina Pai told the Commission that:

> The people of Cork were fantastic. There were priests, nuns, social services workers to help us at the hospital.[145]

Lorna Kelly told the Commission that:

> The Irish people made us feel that it was their tragedy as well as ours. The staff at the Imperial Hotel and at the hospital, as well as the taxi drivers, nuns, and all those that we came across treated us like family.[146]

The deep commitment of the ordinary Irish folk was described by Ramachandra Gopalan in his written statement to the Commission:

> One gentleman, by name Mr. David Twomey, who was at that time president of one of the beer-making companies in Ireland…told my mother, "Don't worry. Consider me your son in Ireland" and voluntarily did all the help. He drove us wherever we needed to go.[147]

---

[144] Testimony of Lata Pada, vol. 1, September 25, 2006, p. 65.
[145] Submission of Zerina Pai, vol. 2, September 26, 2006, pp. 181-182.
[146] Submission of Lorna Kelly, vol. 4, September 28, 2006, p. 432.
[147] Submission and Testimony of Ramachandra Gopalan, vol. 8, October 10, 2006, p. 826.

Susheel Gupta recalled being caught in the rain in Ireland:

> *Neither my father nor I had a raincoat. As we were walking, a group of three Irish people walked up to us, greeted us. We were crying. They hugged us and then took off their own raincoats, handed one to my father as another one of the three individuals put his jacket upon me, buttoned it up, pulled the hood over my head and told me to keep the jacket…I still have the raincoat to this day.[148]*

As Ratheish Yelevarthy said:

> *Motherly understanding and affection were showered on us by the people of Cork…Many Irish families volunteered to put us up in their homes.[149]*

Kalwant Mamak also marvelled at the kindness shown to family members of the victims:

> *…the Irish were the most wonderful people in the world…their hospitality was out of this world.[150]*

Mandip Grewal was a child when his father became a victim. Now married, he attended the memorial in 2005:

> *My wife and I visited Ireland last year for the 20th anniversary and we felt an overwhelming sense of warmth, comfort, belonging and respect that we will never forget. The way in which we were treated and acknowledged compels us to return and visit to Ireland again and again.[151]*

Satrajpal Rai also remarked at the ongoing concern of the Irish:

> *To this day, the people that I met there…offered as much assistance as possible in any which way that we wanted…[152]*

---

[148] Testimony of Susheel Gupta, vol. 2, September 26, 2006, p. 215.
[149] Submission of Ratheish Yelevarthy, vol. 11, October 13, 2006, p. 1051.
[150] Testimony of Kalwant Mamak, vol. 2, September 26, 2006, p. 144.
[151] Submission of Mandip Grewal, Exhibit P-68, vol. 8.
[152] Testimony of Satrajpal Rai, vol. 1, September 25, 2006, p. 102.

The identification of victims' bodies was one of the most difficult tasks for the surviving family members who had traveled to Cork. As Dr. Padmini Turlapati told the Commission:

> All through this, the Irish nurses and nuns were supportive. The local Irish opened their hearts and homes to all of us and brought us flowers, rice, and candles.[153]

Mansi Kinworthy added:

> My father told me that the Irish people were very, very helpful... The people are particularly warm and welcoming. In fact, our family still remains close friends with the Irish nurse who was assigned to us in 1985.[154]

Those brave individuals who undertook the recovery mission have high praise for the Irish people. **Mark Stagg** told the Commission:

> The Irish folk I've met truly know the meaning of kindness.[155]

In the midst of otherwise tragic circumstances, Eric Beauchesne found some solace in the kindness of the Irish:

> The Irish people there were amazing. They took us into their homes literally and they made us feel very welcome and they felt so intimately tied to this tragedy, like it was their tragedy, in a way that I had never seen from any Canadians. It was very touching and it was extremely comforting to me.[156]

In a video submission, Gaurav Gupta told the Commission of the outpouring of love and genuine care of the Irish people:

> The Irish people are so loving, caring and giving. I do not think any other country could have handled it as well as they did...They attend even though they do not know someone on the flight, but still pay their respects to those souls unknown to them. It is just unbelievable...They are truly part of the tragedy.[157]

---

153 Testimony of Dr. Padmini Turlapati, vol. 2, September 26, 2006, p. 194.
154 Statement of Mansi Kinworthy, vol. 4, September 28, 2006, pp. 439-441.
155 Testimony of Mark Stagg, vol. 3, September 27, 2006, p. 347.
156 Testimony of Eric Beauchesne, vol. 6, October 4, 2006, p. 641.
157 Video submission of Gaurav Gupta, Exhibit P-71.

As a lasting testimony of the compassion and support of the Irish community, the first permanent memorial was established at Ahakista on Dunmanus Bay, Ireland.[158]

> I will fail in my duty if I don't mention about the Irish communities' thoughtful action of putting up an Air India memorial, the very same place which is the landfall the plane is supposed to have made it travelled.[159]

The personal and spiritual bond between the Irish and the victims' families continues every year as they assemble on June 23rd to commemorate this tragic event.

As Shipra Rana told the Commission:

> Hats off, really, to the Irish. Such a bond that I think most of us families had built with them. We got so much love from them. It was as though it had just happened in their house, that they were the ones who had lost somebody.[160]

It is difficult to find a silver lining in the midst of such a massive loss of life. Nonetheless, the response of the citizens of Cork, Ireland, and its surrounding communities and the helpfulness of the Irish authorities demonstrated for many the meaning of humanity.

36

---

[158] The Ahakista memorial is described in section IV-B "Memorial Sites".
[159] Submission and Testimony of Ramachandra Gopalan, vol. 8, October 10, 2006, p. 827.
[160] Testimony of Shipra Rana, vol. 7, October 5, 2006, p. 684.

III
THE CANADIAN RESPONSE

Perceived Lack of Support from the Canadian Government

If one theme dominated the family hearings, it was the expression of frustration and disappointment at what the families saw, and continue to see, as the absence of information, moral support, counselling, guidance and general concern from agencies of the Government of Canada. This frustration was heard from family members who appeared at the Commission or submitted written statements. It was a common comment that *nobody from the government ever called us*. Some pointed out the absence of grief counselling services by Canada for the families.

It was evident that the families felt isolated from the government. They often said that they felt that they were not viewed as "real Canadians" and that this was somehow not considered to be a Canadian tragedy. It was common during the hearings to hear expressions of relief from the families that this Commission was created and that their fears and concerns would finally be heard.

Almost to a witness, the family members told the Commission of feeling left out from the beginning of their painful experience. With few exceptions, they wrote or spoke of being ignored –first during the initial period of shock and grief and then later. This section presents a sampling of those views which have been chosen to represent the general sentiments of virtually all families.

On the Scene in Cork, Ireland

Perviz Madon was asked whether anybody from the Canadian government came to her to inquire whether they could help. Her answer: *No, not that I can recall.*[161] She did acknowledge some assistance from Air India while in Ireland. Lorna Kelly said that *the Canadian government was nowhere to be seen.*[162] Kalwant Mamak went into more detail. He told the Commission that:

> We didn't get any information whatsoever, whether it was Air India or any government agency telling us what had happened…there were no Canadian officials.[163]

Kalwant Mamak went on to say that he *was totally lost and there was nobody there to guide me. I couldn't go to the Canadian people because I couldn't find any. I didn't know what to do.*[164]

Haranhalli Radhakrishna said that he did *not meet even a single officer from the Canadian government or the embassy.*[165]

Dr. Padmini Turlapati told the Commission that:

> …we sat without any contact from the government, any social agency or Air India for about four days. The government totally neglected us…[166]

The emotions ran deeper than a sense of being ignored, however. Several witnesses went further, suggesting not simply that Canadian officials seemed absent from the scene, but that they had no interest.

Susheel Gupta was the youngest family member, and only child, on the scene. He told the Commission of his perception that *Canadian government officials did not seem to care at all…Certainly no one in the*

---

[161] Testimony of Perviz Madon, vol. 6, October 4, 2006, p. 598.
[162] Testimony of Lorna Kelly, vol. 4, September 28, 2006, p. 433.
[163] Testimony of Kalwant Mamak, vol. 2, September 26, 2006, p. 143.
[164] Testimony of Kalwant Mamak, vol. 2, September 26, 2006, p. 146.
[165] Submission of Haranhalli Radhakrishna, vol. 9, October 11, 2006, p. 867.
[166] Testimony of Dr. Padmini Turlapati, vol. 2, September 26, 2006, p. 192.

Canadian government stepped up to the plate to assist so that we could all be there together.[167] He recalled hearing his father angrily tell a reporter that:

> *...there was not "one damned Canadian official" here and we were not receiving any support, guidance or information from our own government.*[168]

Dr. Bal Gupta himself said:

> *...there was no emotional, psychological, physical or administrative help or grief counselling or guidance from any government agency.*[169]

Deepak Khandelwal spoke to the Commission about what he perceived as systemic failures:

> *Why were no Canadian officials in Ireland for six days after the bombing to help the families deal with the identification of bodies and related matters? The government at that time was incapable of dealing with this type of a situation.*[170]

He also raised another concern that was echoed by others –the absence of grief counselling services during their darkest hour. He asked why this was not offered to the families at the time of Canada's largest mass murder.[171]

Murthy Subramanian reiterated the apparent absence of counselling and other services, stating:

> *There was no assistance provided to us at Heathrow by the Canadian government, no psychologists, no counsellors. We comforted each other.*[172]

---

[167] Testimony of Susheel Gupta, vol. 2, September 26, 2006, pp. 212-213.
[168] Testimony of Susheel Gupta, vol. 2, September 26, 2006, p. 217.
[169] Submission of Dr. Bal Gupta, vol. 1, September 25, 2006, p. 35.
[170] Testimony of Deepak Khandelwal, vol. 1, September 25, 2006, p. 90.
[171] Testimony of Deepak Khandelwal, vol. 1, September 25, 2006, p. 90.
[172] Submission of Murthy Subramanian, vol. 4, September 28, 2006, p. 415.

Back in Canada

Having returned to Canada to attempt to rebuild their lives and deal with the grief from their sudden and unanticipated losses, the families continued to experience feelings of isolation. Some told the Commission that they perceived covert racism in their attempts to deal with the authorities. Dr. Ramji Khandelwal testified:

> We also started to think that nobody wants to do anything because we are Canadians of Indian origin. We thought at that time, and I think it may be true today too, that it is not taken as a Canadian problem and nobody cares about the lives of Canadians of Indian origin.[173]

Rob Alexander inferred a similar sentiment:

> In particular, there was no form of support from the government or by Air India in the form of grief counselling or other forms of support that could have been useful. If this did not qualify for that type of support, what would a Canadian family have to go through to qualify?[174]

After returning home, the families continued to be disappointed with insufficient or non-existent support from government authorities. Mahesh Sharma said:

> …my biggest problem was that after I lost my family there was no communication with the government. Nothing came…We had no particular support from the Canadian government to counsel us…[175]

Eric Beauchesne articulated the sentiment of many families when he told the Commission:

> I don't think the Canadian government felt any responsibility for helping us in any way, shape or form. We received no contact at all. There was nobody to help us to offer any sort of support, either emotional or logistical. There was no offer to

---

[173] Testimony of Dr. Ramji Khandelwal, vol. 6, October 4, 2006, p. 657.
[174] Testimony of Robbie Mathew Alexander, vol. 5, October 3, 2006, p. 505.
[175] Submission of Mahesh Sharma vol. 5, October 3, 2006, p. 493.

send anybody to Ireland. There was nobody there to call us to offer any kind of counselling at all. I felt they were completely ignorant of any aspect of the impact that this had on the family members.[176]

Mansi Kinworthy noted that, in contrast to the outpouring of support from their extended family, *we did not receive much support from government authorities. No one offered counselling.*[177]

Dr. Chandra Vaidyanathan said that *it is important to emphasize that the Canadian officials and Canada [were] remiss in providing counselling services to the victims' families.*[178]

Ram Gogia remarked that:

> *No Canadian authority contacted me to help me during this confusing and traumatic time... I never received an offer of support or counselling to deal with the tragic loss of my mother from any Canadian official.*[179]

Mandip Grewal said in his submission:

> *It saddens me that there was no support or guidance from the Canadian government for victims' families.*[180]

This sense of a lack of support extended beyond the area of counselling services. In the words of Haranhalli Radhakrishna:

> *In spite of the fact that this was the largest mass murder in the recent times of Canadian history, there were no victim services offered to us. We did not receive any type of counselling to cope with this immense tragedy in our lives. In my case, I did not even receive any assistance from the government in my effort to bring one or two of my nearest family members from India to Canada and immigrate to help me in rebuilding family.*[181]

---

[176] Testimony of Eric Beauchesne, vol. 6, October 4, 2006, p. 633.
[177] Submission of Mansi Kinworthy, vol. 4, September 28, 2006, p. 440.
[178] Submission of Dr. Chandra Vaidyanathan, vol. 6, October 4, 2006, p. 584.
[179] Submission of Ram Gogia, vol. 11, October 13, 2006, pp. 1026-1027.
[180] Submission of Mandip Grewal, vol. 8, October 10, 2006, p. 844.
[181] Submission of Haranhalli Radhakrishna, vol. 9, October 11, 2006, p. 869.

The Ensuing Years

Perviz Madon spoke of the cumulative frustration of family members at the lengthy passage of time from June 23, 1985 until this Commission came into being:

> Just the other day there was a highway that collapsed in Montreal, the overpass. Automatically they're talking of an inquiry. Did anybody have to start lobbying and say, "Hey, we need an inquiry for this"? Pan Am happened two years after us. They had their inquiry right away and we were told because of the criminal investigation that's going to be underway, … we waited for…16 years. So why was it that we were denied this public inquiry for 21 years? Why?[182]

It was apparent that from the date of the Air India bombing until this Commission was created, many family members continued to feel ignored and mistreated. Renee Saklikar said during her appearance:

> My family has put its heart and soul into raising us to view the world as Canadians and yet when we look at the series of failures in relation to this tragedy I think we might ask, well, have we truly been accepted as Canadians?[183]

The feeling that the government did not do enough for the families has created a sense of hopelessness for many individuals. Esther Venketeswaran's view was:

> The way in which this airplane disaster has been handled by the Canadian government has added great insult to injury and fuelled raging indignation. I am part of a losing situation where there is no reward, respect, closure or compensation to make amends for what I have had to endure for a large portion of my life to date.[184]

Satrajpal (Fred) Rai told the Commission that no Canadian dignitary had ever called or written. When asked whether he had ever been contacted by Canadian authorities with expressions of sympathy, he responded:

---

[182] Testimony of Perviz Madon, vol. 6, October 4, 2006, p. 603.
[183] Testimony of Renee Saklikar, vol. 7, October 5, 2006, p. 701.
[184] Submission of Esther Venketeswaran, vol. 9, October 11, 2006, p. 923.

> *No, never. Actually, I'm very, very upset and disgusted, to be honest with you. I thought at the least somebody would call, send a letter. It's almost like we never existed. I'm a Canadian citizen.*[185]

Rama Bhardwaj expressed equal disappointment that *no government official ever showed any support, moral or otherwise. It was unthinkable cold treatment.*[186]

The feeling of neglect extends beyond Canadian borders. Sheila Singh Hanse, whose husband was captain of Air India Flight 182, lives in India, but had similar sentiments:

> *Having been ignored by Air India and the Canadian government for all these years has certainly left my son and myself with the thought of justice delayed is justice denied…*[187]

Sandhya Nil Singh lost her brother, **Surendra P. Singh** (a flight purser), his wife, **Joyosree**, and their infant son, **Ratik**, on Air India Flight 182. She expressed deep concern in her written statement.[188] She failed to understand why Canadian authorities did not consider widely known threats to Air India to be serious during such a volatile political period. She expressed regret about the outcome of the criminal trials, commenting that *an able country like Canada was unable to act in time or give justice.*[189]

Continuing to struggle in coping with their terrible losses, and with raw emotions at the culmination of the British Columbia criminal trial process, the families had a painful reminder of the feelings they had attempted to suppress. Mandip Singh Grewal recalled that day in his written statement to the Commission:

> *As the families were entering the courtroom to hear the verdict, an old man yelled at all of the family members that were present. He told us to go back home, that we were bringing our problems to Canada. This was very hard to hear on such an emotional and anxiety-filled day. To me this is paradigmatic of the way in which this tragedy has been perceived by many in Canada, including*

---

185 Testimony of Satrajpal Rai, vol. 1, September 25, 2006, p. 103.
186 Submission of Rama Bhardwaj, vol. 2, September 26, 2006, p. 157.
187 Submission of Sheila Singh Hanse, vol. 10, October 12, 2006, p. 965.
188 Submission of Sandhya Nil Singh, Exhibit P-88, vol. 11, October 13, 2006.
189 Submission of Sandhya Nil Singh, Exhibit P-88, vol. 11, October 13, 2006, pp. 1032-1033.

government officials; that this was not a Canadian tragedy; that the issues dealt with people involved in a conflict far away. What troubles me the most is the harsh difference in the lack of support I received from my country compared to the immense compassion, sincerity, respect and generosity of the Irish people.[190]

There are striking similarities among the family expressions of concern. They provide, if any was needed, an incentive to examine in detail the way Canadian government institutions responded after June 23, 1985.

---

[190] Submission of Mandip Singh Grewal, vol. 8, October 10, 2006, p. 846.

Canadian Officials

While many victims' family members were critical of the Canadian response after the aircraft went down, the Commission heard from Canadian officials who arrived in Ireland soon after the tragedy. They were well-meaning and well-intended, but unprepared and ill-equipped for what was expected of them. Their numbers and resources were inadequate for what was needed to respond to a terrorist attack of the magnitude of the Air India bombing.

The Commission heard from various Canadian officials who were dispatched to Cork, Ireland in the aftermath of the Air India tragedy. Bob Hathaway, Canada's political officer in Dublin, arrived in Cork from Dublin the afternoon of June 23, 1985.[191] Gavin Stewart was responsible for consular and immigration affairs and Michael Phillips was in charge of political and public affairs at the High Commission in London. Daniel Molgat had been the Assistant Deputy Minister in charge of Europe until two weeks before the bombing. He was in Ottawa prior to an ambassadorial posting to Madrid, when called on June 24th and told that the External Affairs Minister wanted him to proceed to Ireland via London, there being no Canadian ambassador in Dublin at that time. At Heathrow Airport he met Gavin Stewart and Michael Phillips. They travelled together with two family members to Cork.

> When we arrived, one of the first things we did as a group was to go out to the regional hospital and we had a quick briefing on the morgue which had been set up and the way that was going to be organized. We also heard from the person, I think it was the coroner for Cork, who explained that there would be forensic examinations which would take some time and only after those essential legal requirements would the identification process begin. And that meant that there would be a period of some days at least before anything could happen with respect to the people...[192]

The Canadian officials initially relied on the airlines for information on the arrivals of family members, but soon found out that some relatives had arranged their own travel.[193] By June 26th, the Canadian officials had a formal process for being at the airport each time a flight arrived and this was in place until July 12th. The officials wore maple leaves prominently on their lapels and announced that they were present at the airport.[194]

As the enormity of the disaster became apparent, the Canadian contingent was increased to seven. The new arrivals were Scott Heatherington from Canada, Helen Amundsen from the High Commission in London, and Stan Noble, the immigration program manager from Dublin.[195] Daniel Molgat says that with the benefit of

---

[191] Testimony of Daniel Molgat, vol. 13, November 7, 2006, p. 1171.
[192] Testimony of Gavin Stewart, vol. 12, November 6, 2006, pp. 1123-1124.
[193] Testimony of Daniel Molgat, vol. 13, November 7, 2006, p. 1187.
[194] Testimony of Daniel Molgat, vol. 13, November 7, 2006, p. 1184.
[195] Testimony of Gavin Stewart, vol. 12, November 6, 2006, pp. 1129-1131.

hindsight he would have arranged for more people at the outset. Scott Heatherington said that on his arrival on Friday June 28th, he understood that the main concern was to locate the Canadian nationals who were the victims' next of kin and to ask whether there was anything that could be done to help.[196]

During the intense and stressful process of identifying the victims' bodies, the Canadian officials tried to offer comfort. But Irish law required autopsies to be performed before family members were permitted to see and identify victims:

> *Now, that did not go down very well. They found it very difficult, most of them, to understand why they couldn't at least be allowed into the morgue to see the bodies with a view to trying to identify them.*[197]

Essentially, the Canadian officials could do little more than console the bereaved families until the required steps had been completed.

> *…we felt quite bad because there was little you could do to help them in that initial stage other than to kind of listen to them and talk to them and try and see if there was anything you could do, but until the process of identifying the bodies – the remains was set up, they had to wait.*[198]

Some family members expressed frustration to Gavin Stewart that the Irish authorities might not understand the sensitivity of many of the families with respect to burial rites. The Canadian officials were essentially relegated to carrying out immigration-related matters until the identification process began at the hospital.

Daniel Molgat told the Commission of the considerable cooperation the Canadians received from the local police, the hospital, the municipal and county authorities, and the External Affairs Operations Centre in Ottawa. The Irish officials had arranged for social workers to be on-site at the hospital for the families as they arrived to attempt to identify remains. Daniel Molgat says that arrangements were made to make counselling available in Canada through a "hotline" funded by the federal and Ontario governments.[199]

---

[196] Testimony of Scott Heatherington, vol. 4, September 28, 2006, p. 389.
[197] Testimony of Daniel Molgat, vol. 12, November 6, 2006, p. 1144.
[198] Testimony of Scott Heatherington, vol. 4, September 28, 2006, p. 394.
[199] Testimony of Daniel Molgat, vol. 13, November 7, 2006, p. 1170.

David Dewhirst, an immigration officer posted to Bombay, met every incoming plane carrying the remains of the victims. He placed a floral garland on each casket and expressed condolences on behalf of the Canadian government.

Daniel Molgat told the Commission that their work was never compromised by any *latent discrimination or functional discrimination or racism*.[200] He said that he had never worked with a more compassionate team of people, or one that better understood the situation. Most members of the Canadian team had South Asian experience. He says that whatever the faith or ethnic origins of the passengers on Air India Flight 182, this was a Canadian tragedy.[201] He observed that the victims' families were highly educated and seemed to be comfortable dealing with the Canadian officials in English. He thought that they might have found it patronizing to be addressed by Canadian officials in Hindi, Urdu or Punjabi. Gavin Stewart said that the Canadian officials were very conscious of the faith-based concerns of the families, particularly with respect to timely burial or cremation.[202]

It is evident and admitted that the Canadian officials arrived on the scene ill-equipped and too few in numbers to adequately aid the grieving families. Although compassionate and well-intentioned, the officials had limited means and no formal plan of action. They attempted to respond to the emergency as best they could, constrained by local rules governing the victim identification process, restrained as well by a lack of resources. These well-meaning people were placed in an untenable position. They were somehow expected by senior Canadian authorities to respond to this emergency. They were not trained for this task. It was obvious that in 1985 Canada did not have a response team that could react to such a massive and unexpected attack. It was equally evident that those Canadian officials who testified were sincere, and the lingering pain apparent in their testimony speaks highly of them and their good intentions.

The criticisms levelled by victims' family members at officials must be tempered by a number of factors which were outside their control

---

[200] Testimony of Daniel Molgat, vol. 12, November 6, 2006, p. 1147.
[201] Testimony of Daniel Molgat, vol. 12, November 6, 2006, p. 1147.
[202] Testimony of Gavin Stewart, vol. 13, November 7, 2006, pp. 1165-1166.

or beyond their abilities or training. At the same time, the pain and frustration of the family members are real, and their concerns about the apparent absence of support from Canada should not be forgotten. While not seen by all of the families, Canadian officials were in Cork and attempted to assist those family members they could locate.

Over the years, there has been an underlying criticism of the government of that time, and a common expression of disappointment from family members that Prime Minister Brian Mulroney was quick to send a letter of condolence to the Prime Minister of India, Rajiv Gandhi, on Sunday, June 23rd, the day of the attack. The implication was that Prime Minister Mulroney and his government had dismissed this matter as an "Indian tragedy" and by extension minimized Canadian ownership. The Commission heard evidence to the contrary during the hearing.

Testimony during the hearings clarified the sequence of events as follows: Canada's prime minister telephoned his Indian counterpart soon after the tragedy and a letter came from Rajiv Gandhi to Brian Mulroney on June 26, 1985. Prime Minister Mulroney did not write his letter until July 18, 1985.[203] The date of that letter and its filing as evidence before this Commission were confirmed by the Department of the Attorney General and recorded during testimony on May 8, 2007.[204]

In essence, Prime Minister Mulroney noted Canada's grief for the many citizens of both countries who lost their lives in the crash. The bombing had not yet been confirmed. Prime Minister Mulroney went on to say that if this were to be identified as an act of sabotage, Canadian police were fully engaged in identifying and prosecuting the perpetrators. He assured the Indian Prime Minister of full Canadian cooperation in tracking down terrorists within this country and pledged cooperation between the two countries. In closing, the Prime Minister conveyed his own sympathy and that of the Government for the "grievous loss that our two countries have shared."

This information clarifies both the timing and intent of the Prime Minister's letter.

---

[203] Exhibit P-101 CAE 0310.
[204] Confirmation by Mr. Brucker, Office of the Attorney General of Canada, vol. 25, May 8, 2007, p. 2505.

IV
THE AFTERMATH

Continuing Grief

Grief is personal and individuals deal with it differently. Many of the families have attempted to rebuild their lives and find mechanisms to cope with the sudden loss of loved ones. Some have attempted to move on by becoming involved in various activities or absorbed in their work. Others have moved away in the hope of distancing themselves from the painful memories. Still others have dealt with their grief by improving the lot of less fortunate people or have attempted to fill their personal emptiness by participating in activities to support the families in their collective quest for answers, justice or retribution.

Regrettably for some of the families, the murder of a loved one has led to further sorrow through family feuds, financial difficulties, uprooted lives and businesses, sickness and premature death. For these individuals, the tragedy of death has an added companion.

The Commission's Terms of Reference do not include the assessment of compensation. Nevertheless, the testimony of a number of family members mentioned this matter and this report would be incomplete without acknowledging their comments. [205]

---

[205] Among the family witnesses who commented are: Dr. Bal Gupta, vol. 1, September 25, 2006; Zerina Pai, vol. 2, September 26, 2006; Parkash Bedi, vol. 2, September 26, 2006; Mansi Kinworthy, vol. 4, September 28, 2006; Krishna Bhat, vol. 5, October 3, 2006; Promode Sabharwal, vol. 6, October 4, 2006; Upendrakumar Abda, vol. 8, October 10, 2006; Shailendra Gupta, vol. 8, October 10, 2006; Ann Venketeswaran, vol. 9, October 11, 2006; Esther Venketeswaran, vol. 9, October 11, 2006; Neelam Kaushik, vol. 10, October 12, 2006; Sheila Singh Hanse, vol. 10, October 12, 2006; Laxmansinh Abda, vol. 10, October 10, 2006; and Amarjit Bhinder, vol. 11, October 13, 2006.

Compensation was paid only after prolonged civil litigation. The compensation varied in amount for reasons not disclosed to the Commission. Some families reported receiving nothing, whereas others were given cash payments or offers of air travel. Recipients of cash payments told the Commission of very modest settlements in some cases and somewhat more substantial payments in other cases. Even then, in addition to comments on the amount of compensation received, the Commission heard from witnesses such as Mahesh Sharma who urged that families of future victims of terror receive guidance:

> … I understand that it is not in your mandate to award for any compensation, but I think I would like you to mention in your report that in future if such a thing happened…people should be given proper counselling before they sign anything.[206]

---

[206] Statement of Mahesh Sharma, vol. 5, October 3, 2006, p. 496.

Donna Ramah Paul, Upendrakumar Narainji Abda and Laxmansinh Abda

After the loss of the entire **Bhatt** family (see section I-B *Broken Dreams*), the Commission heard from Donna Ramah Paul, Upendrakumar Narainji Abda (**Chandrabala Bhatt**'s brother) and Laxmansinh Abda (**Chandrabala Bhatt**'s nephew) about the impact of that event on their lives:

> *We suffered psychologically. It has taken a long time for us to come to terms with what happened.*[207]

Laxmansinh Abda told the Commission how they questioned the existence of God. He noted the fact that the family had only received the equivalent of $17,000 as compensation in total for the four family members and that no memorial of any kind was established in India. He and Donna Ramah Paul were angry that there was no appropriate contact by Canadian officials in Ireland or later as the investigation proceeded for many years in Canada and elsewhere: *There were no Canadian people to wipe my tears.*[208] While Donna Ramah Paul did get support from her church in Canada and from the people in Ireland for which she was eternally grateful, she felt abandoned by the Canadian government:

> *I don't need your pity. I don't need ... consideration. I don't need your mercy. I want justice from the Canadian government…*[209]

The **Bhatt** tragedy did not end in the waters off the Irish coast. **Chandrabala Bhatt**'s mother sensed that something was wrong at the time of the fateful flight, but because she was bedridden the family did not tell her about the plane crash. Several months later she died, not knowing that her children and grandchildren had perished. The "not guilty" verdict in 2005 merely added fuel to a continuing tragedy, being *a second tragedy for our family heavily scratching their wounds.*[210]

---

[207] Submission of Upendrakumar Narainji Abda, vol. 8, October 10, 2006, p. 812.
[208] Testimony of Donna Ramah Paul, vol. 8, October 10, 2006, p. 804.
[209] Testimony of Donna Ramah Paul, vol. 8, October 10, 2006, p. 783.
[210] Testimony of Laxmansinh Abda, vol. 10, October 12, 2006, p. 996.

After 22 years, many of the **Bhatt** family's belongings are still with Donna Ramah Paul. They are tragic reminders of an ordinary God-fearing family whose lives were prematurely ended: *Simplicity was their way of life, and their belief in God was tremendous.*[211]

---

[211] Testimony of Donna Ramah Paul, vol. 8, October 10, 2006, p. 991.

Parkash Bedi

Parkash Bedi lost his wife, **Saroj Bedi**, his daughter **Anu**, and his son, **Jatin**, on June 23, 1985. Parkash Bedi is haunted by the loss of his entire family and still mourns.

In Ireland after the crash to identify the bodies, Parkash Bedi was in complete denial of his loss. Only when confronted with a photo of his son did the horror begin to sink in:

> *I found my son Jatin's picture and he looked just like he was sleeping, like nothing had happened to him.[212]*

Jatin had been an excellent student, loved sports and always seemed to care about doing the right thing.

Parkash Bedi's wife, **Saroj**, was identified in Ireland by her brother. She was an extremely "caring person" as well as a gifted singer. Just days before the flight she had strange dreams, including one where she was flying like a bird with both her children in her arms and as she told her husband:

> *All of a sudden we are going down and finally fell into a black hole and never came back.[213]*

37-39

Anu, his daughter, had been an A-plus student, a musician and artist, who dreamed of becoming a paediatrician. Because her body was not found, Parkash Bedi continues to believe that she is still alive:

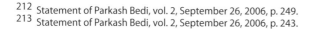

[212] Statement of Parkash Bedi, vol. 2, September 26, 2006, p. 249.
[213] Statement of Parkash Bedi, vol. 2, September 26, 2006, p. 243.

I still have not performed the last rites on my daughter...I believe that she is still alive somewhere.[214]

In fact, he told the Commission that on some days he believes that his daughter might have suffered from amnesia and that she is living in Spain, having been picked up out of the water by Spanish fishermen.

The Air India incident has had a continuing impact on Parkash Bedi. He has seen a series of psychiatrists in trying to deal with the pain of his loss. Often, he has hurt himself physically, adding to the extent of his suffering. His mother moved back to India and stopped eating, often screaming, *Save me, save me, they are trying to kill me. I am drowning.*[215] She died shortly thereafter.

He said at the Inquiry:

It looks like I am living, but I am like a dead body moving around.[216]

---

[214] Statement of Parkash Bedi, vol. 2, September 26, 2006, p. 252.
[215] Statement of Parkash Bedi, vol. 2, September 26, 2006, p. 254.
[216] Statement of Parkash Bedi, vol. 2, September 26, 2006, p. 253.

Mandip Singh Grewal

When **Daljit Singh Grewal** purchased a ticket from Vancouver to India to visit his ailing mother, he felt uncomfortable about travelling because of talk within the community about possible violence against the Government of India. To compound that, his travel agent attempted to discourage him from taking Flight 182 on Air India. Nonetheless, he persisted with his plans because he felt he had to see his mother.

Some 21 years later, his son Mandip Singh Grewal told the Commission of the permanent impact of his loss on their family:

> *The sudden loss of my father was devastating. Words cannot describe the impact his death has had and continues to have on mine and my family's life. My best friend was taken from me in a heartbeat and my whole world was shattered. I was forced to grow up fast and take on many more responsibilities. My mother tried her best to make sure that I could still enjoy life as a child, but the responsibilities were unavoidable.[217]*

The family has attempted to find comfort, but there is lingering sadness. Mandip Singh Grewal's mother now considers flying to be *one of the most dreaded and traumatic experiences*. When Mandip or his sister Prahbjot fly anywhere, their mother is stricken with fear and remains worried until they have arrived safely at their destination.

The gap created by **Daljit Singh Grewal**'s death will not be filled. At the same time, the loss of a father has not diminished his children's positive memories:

> *My father was a compassionate and loving man who believed in truth, loyalty and true friendship. He had the gift of giving without the expectation of receiving anything in return. He was dedicated to his family, friends and work…*

---

[217] Submission of Mandip Singh Grewal, Exhibit P-68, October 10, 2006, p. 843.

He was a devoted and dedicated father to both me and my sister Prahbjot. My father was very proud of us. Whenever possible, he kept me and my sister alongside of him, each holding his hand. He was an outstanding father that always encouraged us children to be confident and excel in all our pursuits.[218]

---

[218] Submission of Mandip Singh Grewal, Exhibit P-68, October 10, 2006, p. 842.

Shipra Rana

Shyla Aurora was a flight attendant on Air India 182. She was described by her sister Shipra Rana as *the light of our lives, just a super, super soul.*[225] *Shyla Aurora* was one of 22 crew members aboard Air India Flight 182.

Shipra Rana appeared before the Commission as a member of the Air India crew members' group and the International Families Group. She explained how she had hosted a party for a number of the Air India crew members and their families on the evening before the flight. Besides her sister, these included *Inder Thakur*, *Priya Thakur*, and their son *Vishal*; *Rima Bhasin*, *Bimal Saha*, *Sunil* and *Irene Shukla*, and *Freddy Balsara*.

> *At that day of the barbecue everyone was relaxed…no talk of politics…no talk about Air India threats. It was just a wonderful evening.* [226]

Shyla Aurora loved her job and went out of her way to make passengers feel at ease.

> *If she served any Sikh she wore her Kara, which is a metal band, which is part of the belief of Sikhism.*[227] *She would purposely make certain that it was visible when she was going to serve.*[228]

The effects on the family after the bombing were enormous. *Shyla Aurora*'s parents, who were considering immigrating to Canada, now refused to come.

> *My dad blamed the bombing on our laws…He never got over it. After my sister, my dad died a bit every day. He used to write and recite poetry. That was his passion. He stopped.*[229]

---

225 Testimony of Shipra Rana, vol. 7, October 5, 2006, p. 676.
226 Testimony of Shipra Rana, vol. 7, October 5, 2006, p. 678.
227 This steel wristband is one of five Sikh articles of faith serving as visible signals of the wearer's commitment and dedication to the order.
228 Testimony of Shipra Rana, vol. 7, October 5, 2006, p. 678.
229 Testimony of Shipra Rana, vol. 7, October 5, 2006, pp. 684-685.

Shyla Aurora's mother was the one who held the family together as they waited for news from the Irish crash site:

> My mother is an incredible woman, very strong, and she just feared something would go wrong with Dad after this. So she held herself back and just kept hugging us and saying 'Pray, pray, pray everything will be okay, don't worry, don't worry, we'll find her'.[230]

Shyla Aurora's body was never found. Her mother has never been the same and still cries at the mention of her daughter. She comes to Canada each year to visit her family. Shipra Rana told the Commission:

> Air India has a policy when an employee…passes away, the parents or the next of kin get free passage for life. So Mom still gets her free passage, two tickets that she uses to come to meet us. And I will and I still fly Air India.[231]

When she flies Air India, Shipra Rana often encounters some of the older crew members at the airport. She asks if they remember her sister, *Shyla* – and they remember her very well.

Shipra Rana said that the families hoped to find the real truth about the bombing of Air India 182.

> You are our last hope. Life here goes on the same. What has changed today? Nothing, except the lives of the families of the Air India victims. All have moved on but us.[232]

---

[230] Testimony of Shipra Rana, vol. 7, October 5, 2006, p. 683.
[231] Testimony of Shipra Rana, vol. 7, October 5, 2006, p. 685.
[232] Testimony of Shipra Rana, vol. 7, October 5, 2006, p. 691.

Chandar Sain Malhotra

Atul K. Malhotra was a young aircraft maintenance engineer working for Indian Airlines, a sister airline of Air India, at the time of the bombing. He was returning to India from Toronto where he had been visiting relatives.

His father, Chandar Sain Malhotra, sent an audio tape to the Commission to provide more information on his son. **Atul Malhotra** was "full of promise" and had "an amazing work ethic". In fact, he was not originally booked on Air India 182 but changed his mind. He arrived after check-in had closed. One of the pilots, a friend of his, permitted his late boarding. Coincidentally, it was the same pilot who had brought him to Canada the previous month!

Atul Malhotra's death weighed heavily on his father. As he said,

> After losing my son suddenly and unexpectedly in the Air India bombing, I was a finished man. …The days were horrible for me, for many, many months – I was not a normal person. I would even cry at my job.[233]

Resigned to honouring his life, not his premature death, on **Atul Malhotra**'s birthday (January 23rd) the family carries out a religious ceremony and offers some puja.[234] Each year on June 23rd Chandar Sain Malhotra makes a donation to a home for orphans and blind children.

---

233 Submission of Chandar Sain Malhotra, Exhibit P-75.
234 A religious ritual performed on various occasions by Hindus to pray or show respect to their chosen deities.

129

Rama Bhardwaj

Harish Bhardwaj was a multi-talented young man with promise. He stood first in his class in music, math, and biology, and graduated with an average of 94.5 per cent. He was accepted into the University of Toronto medical program with a full scholarship.[235] *Harish Bhardwaj* loved music and played the saxophone, drums, trumpet and flute.

43

Harish Bhardwaj was supposed to meet his brother Jatinder and other family members in Delhi. Jatinder Bhardwaj is still having a difficult time dealing with his brother's death.[236] Their father, Parkash, had a heart attack in 1986 from the grief, stress and financial strain. He had traveled to Ireland to identify his son's body which was not found, and was upset at the "unthinkable" treatment from government officials who did not provide any kind of support.[237]

In Canada, *Harish Bhardwaj*'s mother, Rama Bhardwaj, sent a written statement to the Commission. She said her boss told her to take time off to recover from the loss of her son. On her return to work, she *was let go without any reasons*.[238]

At a memorial tree planting at Queen's Park in Toronto in 1987, she told the assembled people how difficult life had been after the

---

235 Submission of Rama Bhardwaj, vol. 2, September 26, 2006, p. 155.
236 Submission of Rama Bhardwaj, vol. 2, September 26, 2006, p. 158.
237 Submission of Rama Bhardwaj, vol. 2, September 26, 2006, p. 157.
238 Submission of Rama Bhardwaj, vol. 2, September 26, 2006, p. 158.

tragedy, that she and her husband were both out of work and on the verge of selling their house.[239]

Rama Bhardwaj felt that some form of racial discrimination might underlie the fact that although highly educated and experienced, she had great difficulty in re-starting her career. She also told the Commission that she sensed that there was some discrimination in how the Air India Inquiry itself was being treated in the media. She wrote:

> *I am offended that the media wants to talk about how much this inquiry is costing. I am a Canadian taxpayer...Why are the Gomery and Arar Inquiries allowed while the Air India Inquiry gets so much criticism? The victims' families are still suffering.[240]*

While courts of law and inquiries continue to search for answers, one thing is certain – **Harish Bhardwaj**, a scholarship student and a future doctor, died prematurely, leaving his family and a nation poorer from his loss.

---

[239] Submission of Rama Bhardwaj, vol. 2, September 26, 2006, p. 159.
[240] Submission of Rama Bhardwaj, vol. 2, September 26, 2006, p. 161.

Sanjay Lazar

Sanjay Lazar lost his father **Sampath Lazar**, his stepmother **Sylvia Lazar** and his young stepsister **Sandeeta Lazar** on Flight 182. His father was an in-flight supervisor that night. **Sylvia Lazar**, an award-winning flight attendant, had recently resigned from Air India and she and **Sandeeta** were along for a holiday. **Sylvia Lazar** was pregnant at the time of her death.

44

Sampath Lazar had worked for Air India for 23 years and was a co-founder of the Air India Cabin Crew Association. Sanjay Lazar said in his written statement to the Commission that his father, a life-long trade unionist, *represented the cause of the downtrodden.*[241]

Sanjay Lazar told the Commission how **Sylvia**, married to his father since 1977, had cared for his ailing younger brother for two years until he died of multiple sclerosis in 1981. **Sandeeta**, his stepsister, was born shortly after that devastating loss.

Life has not been easy for Sanjay Lazar, orphaned suddenly at the age of 17:

> *…I have lived each day of the last 20 years in denial, getting nightmares of what happened.*[242]

While travelling to Ireland to identify the bodies of his family, Sanjay Lazar had a stopover in London, England. At his hotel there was a bomb scare, forcing already distraught families into the pouring rain at midnight and fuelling the grief that had only just started.

Once in Ireland, he encountered further distress. After he thought he had identified the body of his sister **Sandeeta**, another family made a claim that the young child's body belonged to them. To Sanjay Lazar's horror, *the body was handed over to them.* [243] As he said:

---

[241] Statement of Sanjay and Anita Lazar, vol. 10, October 12, 2006, p. 974.
[242] Statement of Sanjay and Anita Lazar, vol. 10, October 12, 2006, p. 978.
[243] Statement of Sanjay and Anita Lazar, vol. 10, October 12, 2006, p. 977.

…her being snatched from the world is the greatest loss that I bear even today.[244]

Back in India and an orphan, Sanjay Lazar was thrown out of the family home in a dispute and had to endure court battles over property and estates, leaving him with *scars that will forever remain.*[245] Air India employed Sanjay Lazar on compassionate grounds following the loss of his family. He has successfully become a full-time member of the airline's flight crew.

In memory of his lost family and all victims, every year on June 23rd obituaries are placed in the *Times of India,* a memorial service is held at his church and funds are given for orphan children to help with their studies. Significantly, although Sanjay Lazar's employment is flying, he will not fly or travel on June 23rd

…as it is a day of penance and prayer for us, a day of remembrance and solemnity.[246]

By Sanjay Lazar [247]

Dad, you were my idol, my hero, and my teacher
Of the righteous truth, my greatest preacher.
Always a friend and more than a mother,
That was my darling Sylvia and none other.

And the greatest love I shall bear alone,
A part of whose life, I have lived and grown,
My dear little Sandeeta, Pebbles –the terrible one,
The void you've created, will be filled by none.

---

[244] Statement of Sanjay and Anita Lazar, vol. 10, October 12, 2006, p. 975
[245] Statement of Sanjay and Anita Lazar, vol. 10, October 12, 2006, p. 973.
[246] Statement of Sanjay and Anita Lazar, vol. 10, October 12, 2006, p. 978.
[247] From *Love, Honour, Respect: The memories of our loved ones,* p. 179.

Satrajpal (Fred) Rai

Satrajpal (Fred) Rai lost his cousin *Kiranjit Rai*. In fact, *Kiranjit Rai* was also his stepsister because in gratitude to *Kiranjit*'s parents for looking after him when he had become ill in his native England, his parents decided to *adopt or sponsor their daughter* [then niece] *to give her a better life* in Canada.[248] Fred Rai told the Commission that as an only child he had always longed for a brother or sister and *Kiranjit* *fit that role perfectly*.

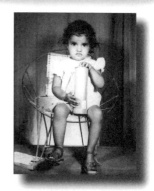

Twelve-year old *Kiranjit* was a good student who had won numerous awards. In fact, she was flying to India as a graduation gift for doing so well in Grade 6. Letters written by her classmates told of a caring, sensitive girl who was helpful to the other students.[249] Fred Rai told the Commission proudly:

> My sister in the matter of two years...for somebody who didn't speak English and came to a new country, she assimilated... exceptionally well.[250]

45-47

Kiranjit's death created enormous guilt for various family members. Fred Rai told how his parents *didn't take it very well at all. They still haven't.*[251] His mother somehow felt responsible for *Kiranjit*'s death and had a nervous breakdown. Shortly after, she was diagnosed with schizophrenia and is still under medical care.

---

248 Testimony of Satrajpal Rai, vol. 1, September 25, 2006, p. 96.
249 Testimony of Satrajpal Rai, vol. 1, September 25, 2006, p. 97.
250 Testimony of Satrajpal Rai, vol. 1, September 25, 2006, p. 97.
251 Testimony of Satrajpal Rai, vol. 1, September 25, 2006, p. 101.

Fred Rai regrets that he never actually said goodbye to **Kiranjit**.[252] He told the Commission:

> For the past several years my life was spiralling out of control due to now what I realize was a lot of guilt that I placed on myself with my sister's passing.[253]

His only real source of comfort is the families of other victims. Fred Rai is a non-practising Sikh who told the Commission he is not very close to his community.

> When I encountered all those family members going through the same grief, it was the first time I actually felt human, felt I was home.[254]

Fred Rai feels that his involvement with the Rae inquiry and now this Commission has helped him to come to terms with himself.

> My involvement in this Commission and with the families has escalated. I finally feel liberated. I wanted to feel human again.[255]

---

[252] Testimony of Satrajpal Rai, vol. 1, September 25, 2006, p. 99.
[253] Testimony of Satrajpal Rai, vol. 1, September 25, 2006, p. 108.
[254] Testimony of Satrajpal Rai, vol. 1, September 25, 2006, p. 104.
[255] Testimony of Satrajpal Rai, vol. 1, September 25, 2006, p. 108.

Zerina Pai lost her brother **Noshir Vaid**, who was the assistant flight purser. They came from a "family of flyers" who all worked for the airline.[256] **Noshir Vaid** had asked for this flight so that he could take his sister on a holiday:

> *My friends in the airline had decided they would all request this flight to take their families on a holiday with them.* [257]

Just before the flight, her ex-husband, also affiliated with Air India, convinced her to see a doctor because she had not been well. She would take a later flight and meet her brother in Frankfurt. This twist of fate has weighed heavily on her:

> *I've had to live with this fact for 21 years. I lost my brother because he left on the flight that was to take me on holiday. My parents reminded me of this constantly.*[258]

Also in her memory are the photo boards that had been put together in the hospital in Cork. On seeing the boards, many family members fainted, cried or fell to their knees. For almost a year, every time she closed her eyes she saw those picture boards.[259]

Noshir Vaid's death was particularly hard on his parents. His mother did not leave her house for 15 years except for temple and funerals, never a wedding or a party. His father lost all interest in his businesses and sold them off, one by one.[260]

Under pressure from Air India accountants to sign a settlement, the bereaved family finally agreed.

> *My parents gave all the money to charity. Once we settled we never again heard from Air India. My parents once asked for tickets to travel to the U.S. to visit my sister. It was refused.*[261]

---

256 Submission of Zerina Pai, vol. 2, September 26, 2006, p. 174.
257 Submission of Zerina Pai, vol. 2, September 26, 2006, p. 176.
258 Submission of Zerina Pai, vol. 2, September 26, 2006, p. 177.
259 Submission of Zerina Pai, vol. 2, September 26, 2006, p. 183.
260 Submission of Zerina Pai, vol. 2, September 26, 2006, p. 184.
261 Submission of Zerina Pai, vol. 2, September 26, 2006, p. 184.

On the occasion of the first memorial service in Ireland, relatives of crew members of Air India Flight 182 were told to fly with tickets from their deceased family members' unused quota from the previous year. Unfortunately, this meant that the family members would have to fly standby. Concerned that they would miss the ceremony, the family members pressured Air India to find them seats on board. Zerina Pai said that for herself and others whose lives had been dedicated to flying, this treatment by their own employer was difficult to accept.

Ann and Esther Venketeswaran

Trichur Krishnan "T.K." Venketeswaran worked for Atomic Energy of Canada (AECL) as an engineer. He had originally come to Canada in February of 1964 as one of 30 young Indian men visiting to learn about the steel industry. When in Welland, Ontario, he was introduced to Ann, a young Canadian registered nurse.

48

Ann Venketeswaran told the Commission that *T.K.* agreed to attend Salvation Army services with her. He continued with his studies abroad, and upon his return to Canada he told Ann that he had embraced Christianity. This was a major change for a man born a Brahman high-caste Hindu.[262] Eventually, *T.K.* married Ann in a Salvation Army church.

Together, they became very involved in church activities and he was constantly learning and studying the Bible. Their faith gave them strength and hope. Ann Venketeswaran told the Commission that she had encouraged her husband to visit India for his brother's wedding and to see his ailing father. He was going to start a new job with AECL upon his return and was close to receiving his professional engineering degree from McMaster University in Hamilton. Everything came to a halt on June 23, 1985:

> Losing a loved one to a terrorist bombing is not the same as losing someone to cancer. It is sudden and unexpected. It is murder, the taking of an innocent life. And for what reason and for why? We just don't understand.[263]

Her world in disarray, Ann Venketeswaran felt extreme guilt, fuelled by her children, who told her that she had sent their father to his death.[264]

> I felt I was to blame, although I cannot explain why. I remember going out and looking up to the sky and feeling so alone. The stars looked like a million pieces of a plane bursting through the sky. I was in shock and felt paralyzed.[265]

262 Testimony of Ann Venketeswaran, vol. 9, October 11, 2006, p. 889.
263 Testimony of Esther Venketeswaran, vol. 9, October 11, 2006, p. 905.
264 Testimony of Ann Venketeswaran, vol. 9, October 11, 2006, p. 898.
265 Testimony of Ann Venketeswaran, vol. 9, October 11, 2006, p. 899.

Ann Venketeswaran undertook a treatment program to deal with her grief, but withdrew after two weeks. She had always relied on her faith as a primary source of healing. She told the Commission that the stigma of being in a treatment program eventually led to the loss of her job as a nurse.

David Venketeswaran was 13 at the time of the bombing. He had a difficult time adjusting to expectations that he could be "man of the house" and hid his sorrow by using drugs. Eventually, David sought help and went through rehabilitation. He graduated in chemical engineering and is currently employed outside this field.

His sister Esther has also had difficulty in dealing with her grief. She read the following text from her victim impact statement prepared for the British Columbia criminal trials:

> I stood on the threshold of adulthood 20 years ago expecting, wanting and waiting to become part of a good world, do good things and have good people in my life who loved me. But June 23rd, 1985 was the day that shattered the end of my peaceful, protected, happy and loving world where I had a mother and a father.[266]

Esther Venketeswaran told the Commission how she worked over the years to ensure that the voices of the victims' families would be heard. She expressed frustration at the lack of official response for a long time. Like her mother, she is grateful for the Salvation Army and the spiritual support they have given.

Esther Venketeswaran told the Commission that after seeing many families share their private grief she eventually saw value in the Inquiry. She continues to struggle with her grief:

> Grief has paralyzed my life, leaving me in an arrested state of development that was never fully realized had my father remained alive. I am intimately acquainted with loneliness and it hurts terribly, more so during the holiday season when it's family time and when I see other families gathered together in various social settings. I feel like a misfit, an outsider and social pariah.[267]

---

[266] Testimony of Esther Venketeswaran, vol. 9, October 11, 2006, p. 923.
[267] Testimony of Esther Venketeswaran, vol. 9, October 11, 2006, p. 925.

Preserving the Memory

In addition to their quest for justice in the deaths of so many innocent people, the families of the victims were intent on ensuring that the memory of their loved ones would be preserved and honoured in perpetuity by memorials and other remembrances. These memorials took the form of public monuments first in Ireland and also in various places across Canada. In addition, the families have established scholarships, awards, sports tournaments and other tributes in their local communities. There are many prayer services which take place each year on June 23rd.

One comprehensive initiative was a memorial book published in 2005 entitled *Love, Honour, Respect: The memories of our loved ones*. The book is referenced in this report. It documents the lives of many of the victims and includes photos, poems, inspirational messages and other touching memorabilia.

As well, a number of other books have been written by journalists and family members. They provide additional background and insights into the lives of individuals affected by the bombing. These must be distinguished from other books and films based loosely on the events of the tragedy. In the latter case, the authors may have used artistic licence to develop stories which are not necessarily based on facts. Whether fact or fiction, whether book or monument, and whether developed by family members or third parties, all of them contribute in some way to keeping the memories alive.

Memorial Sites

Ireland

As previously mentioned, the first physical memorial dedicated to the victims is the dramatic and impressive structure at Ahakista on Dunmanus Bay, Ireland, close to where Air India 182 crashed. Each year families and lately Canadian dignitaries gather on June 23rd to honour the memory of the victims. For many of the families, this is an opportunity to solidify the already strong bonds that have been developed with the local Irish community. Ramachandra Gopalan, who lost his younger brother **Krishnakumar**, told the Commission:

> I do not have any words to describe their generosity, their kindness, especially the nurse who took care of us and even when I went for this memorial -- for the 20th memorial -- she could identify us, whereas we have lost track of the face.[268]

He went on to describe how every year in Ahakista:

> …the children from the school go and play music at the very same time the accident was supposed to have happened, indicated by the sundial there.[269]

49

Canada

In Canada a number of memorial structures have since been or are being built. In addition to memorials in smaller locations like Hagersville, Ontario and Middle Arm, Newfoundland and Labrador, a number of

---

[268] Statement of Ramachandra Gopalan, vol. 8, October 10, 2006, p. 826.
[269] Statement of Ramachandra Gopalan, vol. 8, October 10, 2006, p. 827.

public monuments have been established by the federal government in partnership with the provinces and municipal governments in Vancouver, Toronto and Ottawa, with a fourth planned shortly in Montreal.

On June 23, 2007, 22 years after the destruction and death, a host of dignitaries including Prime Minister Stephen Harper, Ontario Premier Dalton McGuinty and Toronto Mayor David Miller helped dedicate a permanent memorial to the victims along the Toronto waterfront. Family member Lata Pada, reflecting on the moment, said:

> *It was such a serene, beautiful day and somehow it felt that this is a moment of thanksgiving as we finally have a place in Canada that the families of the Kanishka victims can go to, to reflect on those lost souls who touched our lives. You can't but be overwhelmed when you see 331 names etched into the black granite walls. It is no longer a statistic.*[270]

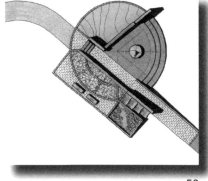

50

Five weeks later, in Vancouver's Stanley Park, another permanent memorial was officially unveiled. At the ceremony, Jayashree Thampi, representing the Air India Victims' Families Association, gave particular emphasis to the 82 children who perished:

> *The memorial wall, etched with the names of the victims, immortalizes the lives lost in this act of terrorism. The children's playground symbolizes the innocence of those children who died in this tragedy. This place offers a beacon of hope to the children of today and the future.*[271]

51

[270] "Kanishka victims finally get a memorial in Canada" by Ajit Jain, June 25, 2007, http://specials.rediff.com/news/2007/jun/25sd1.htm

[271] http://www.cbc.ca/canada/british-columbia/story/2007/07/27/bc-airindiamemorial.htm

In Ottawa, an annual memorial service is held at a monument at Dow's Lake. Ramu Ramakasavan told the Commission:

> By the third anniversary in 1988, my conscience prodded me to try to assist the victims' families in organizing or simply attending the annual memorial at Dow's Lake in Ottawa.[272]

He went on to say that *the annual memorial event included a multi-faith prayer meeting where all religious groups, including Sikhs, were invited.*[273]

While Canada's response was slow, it is commendable that recognition of this Canadian tragedy is now publicly demonstrated.

Tributes and Memorial Services

Many local communities have created tributes to commemorate some of the victims. **Dr. Anchanatt Mathew Alexander** was a respected physician in Hagersville and Jarvis, Ontario. His son told the Commission:

> The communities that he served loved him so much that they organized their own memorial service once they heard the tragic loss of their dear doctor. They also named a nursery of the hospital which he worked at after my father and also planted a tree there in his honour.[274]

Memorial Books

Of all the various memorial books, none is more personal than *Love, Honour, Respect: The memories of our loved ones* released in 2005 by the Family Members of the Victims of Air India Flight 182 and Narita. Led by two family member volunteers, Mona Sandhu of Brampton, Ontario, and Smita Bailey of Edmonton, Alberta, the book (Exhibit P-303), was produced by the British Columbia Ministry of the Attorney General with financial support from the federal Department of Justice.

---

[272] Testimony of Ramu Ramakasavan, vol. 1, September 25, 2006, p. 114.
[273] Testimony of Ramu Ramakasavan, vol. 1, September 25, 2006, p. 117.
[274] Statement of Robbie Mathew Alexander, vol. 5, October 3, 2006, p. 501.

The Honourable Bob Rae told the Commission:

> …it's a magnificent book, which all Canadians should see, in which the lives of the people who were lost are described.[275]

National Day of Remembrance for Victims of Terrorism

The Honourable Bob Rae went on to say that during his inquiry into how Canada should be handling outstanding questions from the Air India bombing:

> I just got a continuing sense that we hadn't … come to grips with this; which is why I came to attach so much importance to the work of memorialization…[276]

Part of that memorialization was the establishment of June 23rd as a National Day of Remembrance for Victims of Terrorism. As Canadians become more aware of the continuing threats of terrorism, the bombing of Air India Flight 182–the most fatal act of terrorism in Canadian history –will be remembered by Canadians hopefully forever.

---

[275] Testimony of the Honourable Bob Rae, vol. 6, October 4, 2006, p. 558.
[276] Testimony of the Honourable Bob Rae, vol. 6, October 4, 2006, p. 558.

Scholarships

As evidenced by many of the families, a large number of the victims had demonstrated academic excellence and were either promising students or at the height of their professional careers. Many of the victims' family members have established scholarships and bursaries as a tribute and to ensure that their hopes and aspirations will live through future generations of students.

Dr. Padmini Turlapati, who lost her sons *Sanjay* and *Deepak*, told the Commission:

> We and all the families started a memorial fund in 2000 and since then the families have been giving scholarships yearly, both in Ireland and Canada.[277]

Parkash Bedi told the Commission that he had established several scholarships in India in memory of his wife and daughter.[278]

Murthy Subramanian established a yearly scholarship award for meritorious students in their final year at an Indian college in memory of his wife *Lakshmi* and his daughter *Veena*, as well as one at *Veena*'s primary school in Canada.[279]

In 1986, the Khandelwal family established two scholarships for female students at the University of Saskatchewan in memory of *Chandra* and *Manju*, one in the College of Pharmacy and one in the College of Medicine.[280]

Dr. Chandra Vaidyanathan said that a scholarship was set up in memory of her brother *Krishnakumar Gopalan* at Carleton University in Ottawa. It is awarded to the best fourth year graduating student in mechanical engineering.[281] Her brother had graduated *with flying colours as the best student in mechanical engineering* from Carleton in 1985.[282] Nothing replaces the loss, but the scholarship is a touching and fitting tribute.

---

[277] Testimony of Dr. Padmini Turlapati, vol. 2, September 26, 2006, pp. 198-199.
[278] Statement of Parkash Bedi, vol. 2, September 26, 2006, p. 257.
[279] Submission of Murthy Subramanian, vol. 4, September 28, 2006, p. 417.
[280] Testimony of Dr. Ramji Khandelwal, vol. 6, October 4, 2006, p. 652.
[281] Testimony of Dr. Chandra Vaidyanathan, vol. 6, October 4, 2006, p. 584.
[282] Testimony of Dr. Chandra Vaidyanathan, vol. 6, October 4, 2006, p. 582.

> At this time of grief it may be some condolence to know that Kris's many friends among students, staff and faculty wish to start a scholarship in his memory. I am currently working on this and I anticipate that it will be known as the Gopalan Award, to go to the highest standing student graduating in Mechanical Engineering.

52

The University of Ottawa established a memorial award in the names of **Rachelle Castonguay** and Dr. Bogdan Zaborski who founded the Department of Geography in 1951. The Zaborski-Castonguay Bursary for Geography Students at the University of Ottawa is awarded annually to an undergraduate student with high academic standing who is participating in northern research through the Department of Geography.

Mahesh Sharma, who lost his wife, two daughters and mother-in-law, established scholarships in Montreal at the Royal West Academy and Elizabeth Ballantyne School where his daughters had attended.[283]Professor Sharma, who has taught at Concordia University for 32 years, recently started three scholarships at Concordia in memory of his wife **Uma** and his daughters **Sandhya** and **Swati**.[284]

Anita Gupta, who lost her sister **Anumita**, told the Commission of finding an album that her mother had put together which contained, among other things, details of all the scholarships and memorials started in her sister's name.[285]

Vipin Bery, who noted that he was still dealing with the fallout from losing his family in the bombing, took pride in a prize established in his daughter **Priya**'s name at her school in Westmount, Quebec, and first attended the awards ceremony in 1986.[286]

Dedicated Careers
A number of victims' family members have chosen to memorialize their lost relatives through their careers. One example is Susheel Gupta who lost his mother **Ramwati**. He told the Commission:

[283] Testimony of Mahesh Sharma, vol. 5, October 3, 2006, p. 490.
[284] Testimony of Mahesh Sharma, vol. 5, October 3, 2006, p. 490.
[285] Testimony of Anita Gupta, vol. 5, October 3, 2006, p. 524.
[286] Submission of Vipin Bery, Exhibit P-38.

Today I'm proud to say that I am a federal prosecutor who does serve the Canadian public working for the department, a position that I consider to be an honour both as a memory to my mother and to all who live in Canada.[287]

Kalwant Mamak, whose wife **Rajinder** died, told the Commission proudly that all of his three children had chosen careers in the field of law enforcement. His son Pal is a police officer in Sarnia and his other son Bob an officer in Ottawa. His daughter Mini in Toronto has a doctorate in forensic sciences and recently gave a seminar on terrorism in Washington to over 300 people. In addition, she spoke at a NATO gathering in Ottawa about terrorism.[288]

Special Events

53-54

A unique memorial is the **Jatin Bedi** Memorial Soccer Tournament in which 12 to 16 high school soccer teams from across India compete.[289] It has grown into a major event and receives coverage in the media. **Jatin**, whose mother **Saroj** and sister **Anu** also died, had been called to compete in a soccer tournament the night before he boarded Air India 182.

55

---

287 Testimony of Susheel Gupta, vol. 2, September 26, 2006, p. 203.
288 Testimony of Kalwant Mamak., vol. 2, September 26, 2006, p. 151.
289 Statement and testimony of Parkash Bedi, vol. 2, September 26, 2006, p. 257.

Rama Bhardwaj, whose son **Harish** was a victim, told the Commission in a written statement that in addition to being a brilliant student who had been accepted to the University of Toronto medical program with a full scholarship, **Harish Bhardwaj** was a long-distance runner who had run in three Terry Fox marathons, the last one in 1984. In his memory, his friend Kevin Leblanc ran the Terry Fox marathon in 1985.[290]

These are examples of the generous actions taken by families and friends to ensure their loved ones are remembered and that hope may displace despair.

---

[290] Statement of Rama Bhardwaj, vol. 2, September 26, 2006, p. 155.

V
RECONCILIATION AND HOPE

Rallying the Families: Seeking Justice

The disorganization that followed the bombing, and the frantic efforts of family members to hurry to Ireland and deal with authorities in the process of identifying the bodies of victims, are well documented. While in Cork, family members recognized the need for "mutual cooperation". Back in Canada, most families felt ignored and had a sense of isolation and hopelessness. In India, other families felt more distanced from the entire matter. Some individuals, well-meaning but without adequate legal or monetary assistance, assumed the challenge of organizing, lobbying for and representing the interests of groups of surviving families. Many of those family members were unable or lacked the confidence to make representations on their own.

These individuals willingly assumed the responsibility to organize and rally others who, like themselves, had been affected so deeply by the loss of Flight 182. Most were related to victims – a few were family friends. All of them have devoted countless hours over the years to ensure that families would be heard and the victims not forgotten.

Dr. Bal Gupta

Dr. Bal Gupta was the first family member to speak before the Commission. He is a driving force behind the Air India Victims Families Association which represents about 80 families covering 180 of the victims of the bombing. One was his wife, **Ramwati "Rama" Gupta**, who died a month before her 38th birthday.[291] She was a pillar of strength for her family. She instilled in her two sons a sense of what was right and a desire to strive to do their best.

She lived every breath of life for her family. Even casual acquaintances were always welcome just like her own family members in her house. To her husband she was a source of unwavering support and wise counsel through thick and thin. She kept her otherwise impatient, excitable and active husband in line by always reminding him to be patient and to smell the roses on the way.[292]

Ramwati Gupta   56

Dr. Bal Gupta has carried that lesson from his wife with him in his pursuit of justice. He remained patient against all odds as he fought to keep the memories alive and to press authorities at various levels for a criminal investigation and a public inquiry. He told the Commission that what has been achieved in recent years was made possible only through the combined efforts of a core group of dedicated people.

While in Ireland, Bal Gupta made a promise to himself to help organize and provide support for the families for as long as necessary. He has been involved for years in meetings, phone calls and conversations during this time. He indicated that the families met frequently at the beginning to discuss concerns and grieve together, and, later on, met whenever necessary. He acknowledges the "mutual cooperation" involved:

---

[291] *Love, Honour, Respect: The memories of our loved ones*, p. 115.
[292] Testimony of Dr. Bal Gupta, vol. 1, September 25, 2006, p. 28.

My special thanks go to those…18 core family members who have volunteered selflessly their emotional strength, time and, yes, money, as needed, to the collective cause continuously through very difficult times from 1985 to today without seeking any limelight or recognition. They are, or in some cases, were, the true leaders. I use the word "were" because some of them have passed away. Let me not forget the second generation of family members who were kids in 1985, children who lost their mother, father, or a sister, or a brother, or a grandfather. They have infused youthful enthusiasm whenever we always falter.[293]

Dr. Gupta served as the Air India Victims Families Association coordinator (and more recently chair) from the beginning. The Association brought families together to deal with government agencies, first in seeking compensation, and then to continue pressing for answers and a public inquiry. He described for the Commission the ongoing cooperation necessary to face the difficult issues and stumbling blocks:

Families have worked very hard to keep together. We were and are a very diverse group brought together by this tragedy… On one hand, this togetherness helped families in coping with the pain and grief … On the other hand, it helped the families in dealing with the government agencies collectively…We kept the whole thing apolitical, demonstrated in front of the Parliament, petitioned the Parliament, got questions raised in the Parliament by members of different political parties. No government official or minister ever contacted any family to communicate about any progress in any investigation for about eight years.[294]

Murthy Subramanian told the Commission:

Bal Gupta organized for the families to meet with a psychiatrist on weekends. Bal Gupta also leads the memorial service that I attend every year on the anniversary.[295]

---

[293] Testimony of Dr. Bal Gupta, vol. 1, September 25, 2006, pp. 26-27.
[294] Testimony of Dr. Bal Gupta, vol. 1, September 25, 2006, pp. 41-42.
[295] Submission of Murthy Subramanian, vol. 4, September 28, 2006, p. 417.

Dr. Bal Gupta told the Commission how all happy occasions have been tainted by an underlying pain and how his wife's parents never recovered from the tragedy. He remarried in 1992 and his new wife has been a source of support and guidance for his sons and their wives. With the cooperation of other surviving families, he continues to work for the families of the victims.

The creation of the Commission of Inquiry gave him renewed hope, but he has guarded optimism for what might result. Dr. Gupta wants the Commission to deal with outstanding issues and make critical recommendations that can control terrorist activities in Canada:

> The Commission's findings and recommendations, if accepted and executed by the government, may hopefully deter some dubious religious preachers from becoming hawkers of hatred and prevent them from turning our houses of worship into temples of doom.[296]

---

[296] Testimony of Dr. Bal Gupta, vol. 1, September 25, 2006, p. 51.

Sundaram Ramakasavan

Sundaram "Ramu" Ramakasavan spoke before the Commission on September 25, 2006. He had no family aboard Air India Flight 182, but a good friend, **Dr. Akhand Pratap Singh**, who perished with his wife **Usha Singh** and their children **Amar** and **Ajai**.[297] **Dr. Akhand Pratap Singh** had come to the University of British Columbia for post-doctoral studies and later was a visiting professor at an Ontario university. He was on his way back to India earlier than planned to accept an academic promotion.

By the third anniversary of the bombing, Ramu Ramakasavan felt that he had to do something to help the victims' families by attending or assisting in organizing the annual memorial at Dow's Lake in Ottawa. He telephoned Dr. Yogesh Paliwal, the primary organizer for the victims' families in the Ottawa region. His son **Mukul Paliwal**, an honours student and a musician, was lost on the flight.[298]

As early as 1988, Ramu Ramakasavan was adamant in pressuring the government to call for a public inquiry and offered to work with Dr. Paliwal in organizing a public demonstration.

> However, I would soon learn that the victim families were in a desperate state and on the verge of giving up their call for justice... The parliamentarians who had promised to raise the issues at the right places had backed off. The RCMP would not talk to any of the victim families, singly or as a group. Finally, they were running out of ideas to continue the struggle in the face of stonewalling by the authorities.[299]

The morning of the scheduled event, Ramu Ramakasavan was wakened by a call from a mutual friend with the news that Dr. Paliwal had died of a massive heart attack during the night:

---

[297] Professor Akhand Singh and his family are listed in Love, Honour, Respect: The memories of our loved ones, p.301. They had no family representation at the hearings.
[298] Love, Honour, Respect, p. 223.
[299] Testimony of Ramu Ramakasavan, vol. 1, September 25, 2006, pp. 114-115.

*Here was the last man standing from the victim families ready
to fight for justice for the victims and he was no more. Despite
the twin tragedies in the short span of three years, Dr. Paliwal's
family decided to go ahead with the demonstration to fulfill his
last wish.*[300]

Persevering throughout the years that followed, and gaining support
from citizens' groups and parliamentarians, Ramu Ramakasavan
fought beside Dr. Bal Gupta, Dr. Ramji Khandelwal of Saskatchewan
and others to gain support to have the criminal investigation reopened
and to keep up the pressure for a public inquiry. He praised the Air
India Task Force established by the RCMP for its professionalism and
compassion in dealing with the families of victims.

*In my opinion, it was an uphill battle. It was very frustrating. It
was demoralizing and knowing that nothing was happening,
we have been -- it may be too harsh…but I think we have
been lied to…misled by everybody who talked to the families.
Again and again and again, we were told that there is an
active criminal investigation going on. Later on we found out
nothing was happening. We were told by not only politicians
but bureaucrats, RCMP, everyone, they just I think lied to us,
misled us, so that we keep quiet.*[301]

Ramu Ramakasavan refused to retreat from his mission to create
momentum for a public inquiry, even after the acquittal of those
charged in the criminal trial:

*…whether we wanted to fight for justice or not, the people at
large, even people who are not East Indians, wanted us to fight.
They had empowered us to fight. They would do anything to
support us so that we would continue to fight. So giving up
and walking away would be my personal failure.*[302]

In the face of ongoing frustration, refusals to meet, perceived and
real threats to his safety and enormous time requirements, Ramu
Ramakasavan persevered in his quest to see this Commission of
Inquiry established.

---

[300] Testimony of Ramu Ramakasavan, vol. 1, September 25, 2006, p. 116.
[301] Testimony of Dr. Ramji Khandelwal, vol. 6, October 4, 2006, p. 656.
[302] Testimony of Ramu Ramakasavan, vol. 1, September 25, 2006, p. 134.

Overcoming Grief to Create a Better World

Out of the ruins of the Air India tragedy, family members sought mechanisms to cope with their losses. Some did not succeed and died prematurely with the pain unabated as a consequence of their inability to accept such grief. A number of family members continue to grieve and to seek relief; others hover on the precipice of despair. However, faced with the reality that loved ones were gone, many found the strength and determination to pursue a path of good works and charity. Their efforts to help others through volunteer activities, medical clinics, teaching and other forms of giving are described in this section.

Dr. Chandra Sankurathri

Manjari Sankurathri was flying to India with her six-year-old son *Srikiran* and her three-year-old daughter *Sarada*. They were going to attend the wedding of *Manjari Sankurathri*'s brother in August. *Manjari Sankurathri*'s husband, Dr. Chandra Sankurathri, was a biologist working for Health and Welfare Canada who had stayed behind to work, intending to join them in July. They planned to return home together before the school year commenced in September.

57

For three years after the bombing, Dr. Chandra Sankurathri continued to work in Ottawa while struggling with the memories of his lost family. He concluded that the only way to restore meaning to his life was to return to India and begin a mission to help those less fortunate than he:

> *First of all, my reaction was disbelief. I did not believe that … it happened … So it took me almost three years to erase what had happened, and I studied a lot to cope…because it was not really easy. That was the most difficult part of my…whole life; and finally I have decided… to find something meaningful for my life…I had to be productive… so that I could be useful to other people. With that intent, I left this country in 1988, to start working with the people, mostly children, in India.*[303]

---

[303] Testimony of Dr. Chandra Sankurathri, vol. 44, June 18, 2007, p. 5343.

Dr. Chandra Sankurathri resigned his public service employment, liquidated everything of value, including his federal pension, and established a Canadian-registered charitable foundation named in his wife's memory (the **Manjari Sankurathri** *Memorial Foundation*). He opened a school in 1992 to provide education for poor children. The school, **Sarada** *Vidyalayam*,[304] named for his daughter, is located in the small Indian village of Kakinada in the state of Andhra Pradesh where he and his wife were born. Schooling from Grades 1 through 7 is provided without charge to all children living in the area.

58

Dr. Sankurathri told the Commission that the school has achieved enormous success and that not one student has dropped out:

> *Since the last 15 years we did not see a single student drop out of education. They all completed their high school diplomas and also attended college. Some of them have graduated from the college and [are] working in our own foundation now.*[305]

Consideration is being given to expanding coverage to high school grades in order to allow youth to complete their education without having to move away.

His son **Srikiran** dreamt of becoming a paediatric ophthalmologist when he grew up –an admirable vision for a boy of six.[306] In his memory, Dr. Chandra Sankurathri established an eye hospital in the same compound as the school. The **Srikiran** *Institute of Ophthalmology* provides equitable, accessible and affordable eye care to everyone in the region:

---

[304] "Vidyalayam" is the Sanskrit word for "school".
[305] Testimony of Dr. Chandra Sankurathri, vol. 44, June 18, 2007, p. 5345.
[306] *Love, Honour, Respect: The memories of our loved ones* , p.275.

…blindness is very prevalent especially in the rural areas where there are no eye care facilities …almost 80 per cent of the blindness is either preventable or curable… for cataract blindness. It hardly takes three to four minutes of a surgeon's time. So this kind of blindness is not needed in the community, so we are planning to go to

59

the villages and try to identify people with cataract blindness restoring eyesight for them… We also screen children for eye problems, so that…in a timely intervention…you can prevent the blindness also.[307]

The hospital sees about 300 outpatients daily and offers surgery to correct cataracts, glaucoma, corneal and retinal problems. The hope is to reach people who might otherwise be unable to access such care. In addition there is a special paediatric eye care unit. Dr. Chandra Sankurathri estimates that about 12,000 surgeries are performed each year. The Canadian International Development Agency (CIDA) is an official supporting organization and various Canadian health agencies have provided funding to help in this noble work. Several physicians from the University of Ottawa Eye Institute, among others, have volunteered to go to Kakinada to assist, operate and help to train the local doctors.

This is an inspiring story of how a man dealt with grief by rebuilding his life to help so many people overcome illiteracy and eye disease. Only 10 percent of the patients are able to pay fees of up to what Canadians may view as a modest $300. Ninety percent of his patients at the clinic and students at the school are charity cases. Somehow, Dr. Chandra Sankurathri's foundation is able to deliver both its educational and medical services to everyone on a modest budget of $500,000 annually.

---

[307] Testimony of Dr. Chandra Sankurathri, vol. 44, June 18, 2007, p. 5346.

Lata Pada

When Lata Pada lost her husband **Vishnu Pada** and daughters **Arti** and **Brinda** in the bombing of June 23, 1985, *a horrific and unimaginable darkness engulfed me.*[308]

Brinda was 18 and had graduated from Grade 13 the night before the scheduled flight to India:

> *Photographs of Brinda excitedly celebrating her graduation are forever seared in my memory. Her dreams of a life ahead are now buried with her in the ocean bed of the Atlantic.*[309]

Her second daughter **Arti** was 15 years old and:

> *… brimming with aspirations of being a doctor, the clown of her class, an affectionate and doting daughter, the popular babysitter on our street, training to be a swimming coach…Her loyalty and support to her friends made her a very special person.*[310]

The girls loved India and Indonesia, where their father was transferred by his employer from Sudbury, Ontario to work in the company's nickel mining operations on the island of Sulawesi. **Vishnu Pada** was, according to his wife, a "quintessential Canadian" and a very special man. He was an accomplished geologist, a folk singer, had a great sense of humour, and was a lover of Canadian winter activities –skiing, ice-fishing and curling. He was also a fan of tennis and cricket. He was a man of many cultures and a champion of multicultural and interfaith activities:

> *Vishnu was a man with a vision for a better world, always believing in his capacity to make a difference. I was always filled with admiration for his passion for volunteer work such as visits to senior citizens' homes and hospices for the terminally ill.*[311]

---

[308] Submission of Lata Pada, vol. 1, September 25, 2006, p. 53.
[309] Submission of Lata Pada, vol. 1, September 25, 2006, pp. 59-60.
[310] Submission of Lata Pada, vol. 1, September 25, 2006, p. 60.
[311] Submission of Lata Pada, vol. 1, September 25, 2006, p. 57.

Lata Pada is a classical dancer. In June 1985, she had gone to India two weeks in advance of her family to rehearse for a summer performance. ***Vishnu Pada*** was always supportive of his wife's involvement in artistic endeavours…

> *encouraging me to explore my potential as a classical dancer. He understood my need to define my own identity, giving me the space and independence to pursue my academic and artistic interests.[312]*

Lata Pada told the Commission that her loneliness will never go away and that she has an inner sadness at the prospect of never again hearing her husband say "I love you", or dreaming of holding grandchildren in her arms. At the same time, she has been able to recapture her own life from the void created by the murder of her family by immersing herself in dance:

> *…the events of 1985 marked the beginning of a journey of deep personal and spiritual transformation, a journey that would in time reveal dance as the metonymy of my existence and a return to wholeness. My life in dance became a pilgrimage, a sacred pathway towards a new revelation of my inner being.*
>
> *As I danced the poetry of India's great saint poets, I came to understand the philosophy of my faith and the profound truths of the cyclical nature of life and death. I came to comprehend the significance of the Holy Scriptures of Bhagavad Gita of self-realization and the purpose for human existence. I went back to school and I did my master's in dance at York University in 1996.[313]*

Having found inner strength through dance, Lata Pada was able to become a public voice for the victims of Air India Flight 182. Often she would work with politicians, journalists and ordinary Canadians to raise their awareness of the impact of the 1985 terrorist attack on those left behind, and about remedies that should be pursued to avoid a reoccurrence.

---

[312] Submission of Lata Pada, vol. 1, September 25, 2006, pp. 56-57.
[313] Submission of Lata Pada, vol. 1, September 25, 2006, pp. 69-70.

We cannot allow history to repeat itself. We have been patient, dignified and hopeful, while coping with an unimaginable pain that the rest of Canada has forgotten about. Twenty-one years ago, a devastating tragedy irrevocably altered all our lives and the one hope we held on to was the successful conviction of the two accused. The long and expensive trial was yet another callous miscarriage of justice.[314]

Despite many setbacks and disappointments, Lata Pada continues to advocate on behalf of the families of the victims and left the Commission to ponder the summation of her pain:

Imagine knowing that there will never be closure. Imagine living with the pervasive and lingering sadness for the rest of your life. Imagine facing happiness with the inevitable "if only". Imagine not ever seeing them again. Imagine never feeling complete again.[315]

60

---

314 Submission of Lata Pada, vol. 1, September 25, 2006, p. 75.
315 Submission of Lata Pada, vol. 1, September 25, 2006, p. 71.

Susheel Gupta

Susheel Gupta was 12 years old when his mother **Ramwati Gupta** boarded Flight 182. The news of the crash and her death devastated him and created feelings of guilt:

> At 12 years old, what could I think and feel but guilt that my mother was blown up and murdered alone instead of all of us being together or instead of it being me? To this day I still ask myself these questions and think these thoughts no matter how illogical they are. Emotion does not always coincide with logic.[316]

61

Susheel Gupta did not comprehend the meaning of death at the age of 12, but understood that he would never see his mother again. Amidst a flurry of activity at home, with relatives and friends coming by to console the family, he left the house to complete his paper route. He cried the entire time. At the end of his deliveries, he saw a turtle, overturned and struggling. His first instinct was to hit the helpless turtle. But then, his thoughts turned to how his late mother, through no fault of her own, had been ripped away forever by evil forces:

> It's like I had an epiphany right then and there with that turtle…I decided I wasn't going to be part of that evil, that I was going to try to be on the side of good for the innocents in our world. I walked over to the turtle, lifted it up, placed him on his feet towards the water, sat back down and watched as it slowly made its way towards the water safely. And then with that epiphany, I got on my bike, went home feeling angry but at least feeling a little more filled with purpose.[317]

Soon after that, the Guptas were advised that a chartered plane would take up to two members of each family to Ireland for the identification of bodies. Susheel was 12, but his father had little choice and took him, leaving his almost 18-year-old brother Suneel alone at home. Susheel

---

316 Testimony of Susheel Gupta, vol. 2, September 26, 2006, pp. 206-207.
317 Testimony of Susheel Gupta, vol. 2, September 26, 2006, p. 211.

168

Gupta was the only child who went to Ireland in the aftermath of the bombing.

The activities of the following days had high and low points. The kindness and warmth of the local citizenry are etched in Susheel Gupta's memory. But so are the images of dead bodies he found lying behind closed doors in the Cork Regional Hospital:

> *I was 12, looking at all these dead bodies. I left only because of the fear of getting in trouble from my father for being somewhere where I shouldn't have been. As I looked at those bodies, I remembered the turtle back home. The faces of those bodies are still burning in my head today. I picture them almost every day, every night, before I go to sleep, sometimes while I'm sitting at work.[318]*

After Ireland he travelled to India for the cremation of his mother's body and participated in lighting matches for cremation, all of which took a toll on young Susheel. Six months after returning to Toronto, he was hospitalized and in isolation with an illness that continues to flare up. His physicians attribute the ailment to the cumulative trauma of the events beginning with his mother's death and her cremation.

Susheel Gupta rose above his personal suffering to pursue a course of action to make his late mother proud. He volunteered with community organizations and took his studies more seriously. As noted earlier (see section IV-B *Dedicated Careers*) he decided to purse a career in law and to work on the side of justice:

> *I promised myself and to my mother that I was going to work in a field where I could make my country, Canada, safer, healthier and happier, and that decision turned into my decision to be a lawyer, for I personally believe it speaks to the fact that I hold great respect for the Department of Justice and our government institutions, even being a victim of terrorism, where there have really been no convictions. I could not walk into a court of law today if I did not have faith in our laws and our justice system.[319]*

---

[318] Testimony of Susheel Gupta, vol. 2, September 26, 2006, p. 218.
[319] Testimony of Susheel Gupta, vol. 2, September 26, 2006, p. 225.

When he appeared before the Commission, Susheel Gupta was a federal Crown prosecutor. He spoke with pride about his close friendships with law enforcement officials, members of the Bar and judges, all of whom are part of the Canadian system of law enforcement and the pursuit of justice. In spite of his personal tragedy, Susheel Gupta told the Commission that he considered it an honour to be a participant in the institutions reflective of Canada's system of justice.

Kalwant Mamak

Kalwant Mamak is a Canadian Sikh living in Sarnia, Ontario. He came to Canada in 1970, first working for a tool and die company in Chatham, Ontario. Within two years he had started his own women's clothing and accessories store in Chatham. In a few years, he had moved to the wholesale market and operated four stores in Ontario. His wife **Rajinder Mamak** and two young children had joined him by then and she managed their store in Sarnia. As Kalwant Mamak recalled, **Rajinder** was a kind wife, a caring mother and a partner beyond his expectations.

Rajinder Mamak   62

Rajinder Mamak was going to India for three weeks to visit her ailing father. The entire family was planning to go there for a winter vacation. Their elder son Pal, a shy teenager, did not want to hug his mother as she left because, as he said, *Mom, you are just going for three weeks. You'll be back.*[320]

After the identification of her body in Ireland, Kalwant Mamak made what he described as the biggest mistake of his life. On the advice of his wife's relatives in India, he did not take her body there for cremation, but went with **Rajinder**'s brother to London, England where her body was cremated. His children still question him on why they never had a last opportunity to see their mother's face. It is an unfortunate twist of fate that his hope

---

[320] Testimony of Kalwant Mamak, vol. 2, September 26, 2006, p. 140.

of doing the right thing was not shared by others close to him.

In Sarnia, the small local Sikh population and other friends in the community had made arrangements for a memorial service.

His wife's death left a void in the family. Everyone was deeply dependent on her for all aspects of the household, particularly the preparation of meals which he wistfully recalled:

> *It was the most difficult years of my life. I didn't want my children to stray. I was always there for them. We were having McDonald's every day. We don't know how to cook. When we came home, my children would ask, "Pa, not McDonald's today. Can you make us supper?" I said, "I don't know how to cook. We'll try it." We used to try and then the things would go bad and something would go wrong with it and then we would end up again in a fast food restaurant.*[321]

Being a single father and running his businesses proved too stressful. He suffered a major heart attack on June 23, 1987, but is grateful for his recovery and for what his children have become. Although they suffered from the Air India tragedy and had little help from any government agencies, all three of Kalwant Mamak's children now have careers in the field of law enforcement (see section IV-B *Dedicated Careers*).

Kalwant Mamak went to India and successfully learned how to cook. Today, he volunteers his services to cook for charitable and fundraising events. His mission is to help others wherever the opportunity arises:

> *… I cook for charities now. We did it for the Iran earthquake. We cooked for 500 people. Then we cooked for the tsunami dinner…We did it for the Cancer Society…We do a voluntary job…*[322]

---

[321] Testimony of Kalwant Mamak, vol. 2, September 26, 2006, pp. 149-150.
[322] Testimony of Kalwant Mamak, vol. 2, September 26, 2006, pp. 151-152.

Jayashree Thampi lost her husband **Kanaka Lakshmanan** [323] (**"Babu"**) and daughter, **Preethi**, on Flight 182.

Babu Lakshmanan was an engineer who had an easy and jovial disposition. He moved to Canada in 1976 with his wife. Their daughter **Preethi** was seven years old, "vivacious and full of life". As her mother told the Commission:

> She was very pretty…loved to dance, particularly Indian classical dancing, and she loved music.[324]

Babu Lakshmanan and **Preethi** were travelling to India for his niece's wedding. Because she did not have sufficient holiday time, Jayashree Thampi planned to join them a couple of weeks later. When she heard of the loss of her husband and daughter, she was unable to cry. In fact, as she told the Commission, she pretended that nothing had happened to her.

> For many months I hoped somebody would have rescued Babu and Preethi and would imagine getting calls from them.[325]

Her inability to cry lasted 20 years. On August 2, 2005, her son was on board an Air France plane that skidded on the runway and burst into flames at Pearson International Airport in Toronto. Miraculously there were no fatalities.

> Nobody understood why I was crying because my son was safe. They didn't know I was not crying for the son who made it but for the daughter who didn't. For the first time in 20 years I mourned the death of my daughter and cried for her.[326]

---

[323] The full name of Mrs. Jayashree Thampi's deceased husband appears in *Love, Honour, Respect*, 2005, p. 173.
[324] Statement of Jayashree Thampi, vol. 2, September 26, 2006, p. 164.
[325] Statement of Jayashree Thampi, vol. 2, September 26, 2006, pp. 167-168.
[326] Statement of Jayashree Thampi, vol. 2, September 26, 2006, p. 168.

Jayashree Thampi told the Commission that after the Air India bombing in 1985, nobody from the Canadian government called and *there was no offer of counselling from Air India or the government.*[327] In contrast, after her son's accident in 2005:

> *Air France offered counselling to my family and I accepted the offer. The therapy allowed me to start dealing with the issues I had never dealt with before.*[328]

As a result of this "therapeutic experience", Jayashree Thampi was able to become an active member of the committee responsible for establishing memorials for the Victims of Air India Flight 182 in Toronto and Vancouver.

---

[327] Statement of Jayashree Thampi, vol. 2, September 26, 2006, p. 168.
[328] Statement of Jayashree Thampi, vol. 2, September 26, 2006, p. 168.

Anita Gupta

Anumita Gupta was 16 years old when she boarded Flight 182. Her sister Anita was 11. Anita Gupta told the Commission that she felt a sense of abandonment when she was left behind with family friends while her parents went to Ireland to look for **Mita**'s body.[329] Then, in her words, she felt a "sense of false elation" when her mother phoned from Ireland in the middle of the night:

> … to tell me that they had found my sister. I remember feeling so happy for an instant that she had been found and this whole nightmare was over, before it hit me that it was just her dead body, it wasn't her.[330]

She told the Commission that she remembers most about her lost sister *how meaningful her friendship had been to many people and how she knew how to be a true friend…*

> The stolen opportunity to become friends with my sister is my continuing loss… we would have had so much time as we grew up together and celebrated with each other the joys of life, like our weddings, choosing our careers, raising our children, as well as supporting each other through the sadness, such as the deaths of my parents.[331]

Anita Gupta is now a clinical psychologist. She shared with the Commission her personal and professional opinions on the continuing need for contact among the victims of violence and terrorism, as the grief is constant or recurring:

> A lot of times in the initial impact of an event like this, you are so busy with doing all the things that need to be done; identifying bodies, signing wills… and so it's so important to contact victims of violent crime and terrorism in the ensuing months, maybe on the year anniversary, having available phone numbers where people can contact, should they feel it, because it might just be one lonely night that they decide to call. They are not always going to… say "yes" even if they need it when someone approaches them, because it might not be the right time.[332]

---

[329] Statement of Anita Gupta, vol. 5, October 3, 2007, p. 512.
[330] Statement of Anita Gupta, vol. 5, October 3, 2007, p. 511.
[331] Statement of Anita Gupta, vol. 5, October 3, 2007, p. 512.
[332] Statement of Anita Gupta, vol. 5, October 3, 2007, p. 523.

She initially found it difficult through adolescence to think of **Anumita**'s death as a murder. The full realization finally came while at university and charges were laid in British Columbia. She told the Commission that the disappointing outcome of the criminal trials awoke something that had been dormant within her. She became more involved with other family members and joined in the effort to create pressure for a public inquiry.

For the first time, she attended the memorial service in Ireland on the 20th anniversary of the bombing and there met other family members who had grown up with similar losses.

Another transformation took place in Anita Gupta. While growing up, she disdained members of the media:

> ... I remember thinking of the press as vultures, creatures who swooped down on our family every June 23rd... so my parents could speak of the loss of their daughter and my father could express his frustrations, anger and bewilderment at the lack of prosecution, as well as government response to the bombings. I remember running to my friend's house on many occasions so that I could avoid the reporters' visits...[333]

She told the Commission that her mother would sometimes stop her father from speaking to reporters because it upset Anita so much.

She wondered how her late father would react to hearing her say things today that he had said 20 years ago. Through her involvement with other family members and her active participation in the public policy process, Anita Gupta now appreciates the media for keeping the Air India story alive and not abandoned to history:

> Today, I feel a deep sense of gratitude towards members of the press for keeping the story alive year after year, even when it was considered old news. I frankly don't know where we would be without the press, but I didn't always feel that way.[334]

---

[333] Statement of Anita Gupta, vol. 5, October 3, 2007, pp. 524-25.
[334] Statement of Anita Gupta, vol. 5, October 3, 2007, p. 524.

VI
CONCLUDING STATEMENT

The first stage of hearings concluded on October 13, 2006 with the following statement by the Commissioner:

> ...we are at the conclusion of Stage 1 of the inquiry. It would be remiss on my part if I did not express thanks to family members who, with great sacrifice emotionally and physically, appeared to give evidence, to express some amazement that the families have managed to stay in substantial contact over many years of disappointment and grief. Their participation, I think, contributed to the knowledge of the Canadian people as to the immense nature of the tragedy. I think too we should express our gratitude to the Irish and other rescuers who came and gave evidence. We thank them for that and, of course, we thank them for their efforts in the rescue attempts that they made. It is also noteworthy and should be part of the record that to a person every family member who visited Cork for the purposes of identifying bodies and other tasks were all impressed by the compassion and generosity shown to them by the Irish people.
>
> In summation, what we have heard to date has been valuable to the Commission and to the country. It has promoted a better understanding of the tragedy experienced by the families and those who worked to recover the bodies lost in the bombing. The Commission is, of course, aware that while we now have a better understanding, only those persons who lived and continue to live the tragedy and its aftermath can truly feel the impact of this act of terrorism.[335]

There are no recommendations associated with the first stage of the Inquiry.

---

[335] Vol. 11, October 13, 2006, pp. 1041-42.

In Memoriam

Aggarwal, Rahul
Ahmed, Indra & Sarah
Alexander, Dr. Anchanatt Mathew
Alexander, Simon, Annamma, Reena & Simon Jr.
Allard, Colette Morin
Anantaraman, Bhavani, Aruna & Rupa
Asirwatham, Ruth, Sunita & Anita
Aurora, Shyla
Bajaj, Anju
Balaraman, Saradambal & Narayanan (Rodger)
Balasubramanian, Ramachandran
Balsara, Freddy
Beauchesne, Gaston
Bedi, Saroj, Anu & Jatin
Berar, Jogeshwar Singh
Berry, Sharad
Bery, Neelam, Priya & Aditya
Bhagat, Adush
Bhalla, Nirmal, Manju & Dalip Kumar
Bhardwaj, Harish
Bhasin, Rima
Bhat, Muktha & Praveen Deepak
Bhat, Parag Vijay, Chand Motiram & Siddhant
Bhatt, Vinubhai, Chandrabala, Bina & Tina
Bhinder, Capt. Satwinder Singh
Bisen, Leena Deep
Castonguay, Rachelle
Chandrasekhar, Sukumar
Chatlani, Nita, Mala & Marc Charles
Cheema, Shingara Singh

Chopra, Jagdish & Shampari

Chug, Ratna Kaur

Daniel, Varghese, Celine, Ruby Ann & Robyn

Das, Ruby, Anita & Arindar

DeSa, Anthony Sebastian

deSouza, Ronald

Dhunna, Bhagrani, Shashi, Rajesh & Suneal

Dinshaw, Jamshed & Pamela

Dumasia, Dara Dinshaw

Enayati, Ardeshir

Furdoonji, Homai

Gadkar, Anita

Gambhir, Santosh, Angeline & Julie

Gaonkar, Shyama

Ghatge, Sangeeta

Gogia, Bhagwanti

Gogne, Ritu

Gopalan, Krishnakumar

Gossain, Kalpana, Aparna & Arun

Grewal, Daljit Singh

Gupta, Anumita

Gupta, Ramwati

Gupta, Shashi

Gupta, Santosh

Gupta, Shashi, Arti & Amit

Gupta, Rajesh, Swantantar, Vandana & Vishal

Hanse, Captain Narendra Singh

Harpalani, Rashmi, Deepa & Sumanta

Jacob, Bulivelil Koshy, Aleykutty, Jissey, Jancey & Justin

Jain, Om Prakash, Rani Indu, Ruchi & Rikki

Jain, Anoopuma

Jaipuria, Mala

Jalan, Devkrishan, Shila, Anita & Vinay

James, Annie Josephine

Jethwa, Dr. Zebunnisa & Dr. Umar

Job, Aleykutty & Teena

Jutras, Rita

Kachroo, Mohan Rani

Kaj, Leena Fatej

Kalsi, Indira

Kammila, Rama Devi

Kapoor, Santosh, Sharmila & Sabrina

Kashipri, Neli & Athikho

Kaur, Gurmit

Kaur, Parmjit

Kaushal, Bishan Ram

Kelly, Barsa

Khan, Rahamathulla

Khandelwal, Chandra & Manju

Khera, Suman & Rashi

Kochher, Sandeep

Kumar, Manju & Kevin

Kumar, Ramachandran

Kumar, Chitra

Lakshmanan, Kanaka & Preethi

Lasrado, Sharon

Laurence, Shyamala & Krithika

Lazar, Sampath, Sylvia & Sandeeta

Leger, Father Joseph

Lougheed, Donald George

Lulla, Monish

Madon, Sam H.

Mainguy, Lina

Malhotra, Atul K.

Mamak, Rajinder

Manjania, Nasib

Marjara, Davinder & Seema

Martel, Alain

Mehta, Kishor, Chandralekha, Nilesh & Neesha

Merchant, Natasha

Minhas, Balwinder Kaur & Kulbir Kaur

Molakala, Prabhavathi

Mukerji, Nishith & Shefali

Mukhi, Renu

Mullick, Deepak

Murthy, Susheela, Bhavani & Narayana

Murugan, Gnanendran, Sumithra, Lavanya & Ramya

Nadkarni, Deven & Rahul

Pada, Vishnu, Brinda & Arti

Paliwal, Mukul

Patel, Babubai

Patel, Bipan Kumar

Patel, Marazban

Patel, Mohanbhai

Phansekar, Rita

Puri, Veena, Ashu & Amit

Quadri, Syed Qutubuddin, Shaiesta, Rubina, Arishiya & Atif

Radhakrishna, Nagasundara, Jyothi & Thejus

Raghavan, Suseela

Raghuveeran, Vasantha & Rajiv

Rai, Kiranjit Kaur

Ramachandran, Pratibha

Ramaswamy, Janaki

Rauthan, Budhi & Pooja

Rodricks, Elaine

Sabharwal, Meghana

Sadiq, Dr. Sugra

Sagi, Sujatha, Kavitha & Kalpana

Saha, Bimal Kumar

Sahu, Ram, Pradeep K. & Pushpa

Sakhawalkar, Dattatraya, Usha, Sanjay, Surekha & Sunil

Sankurathri, Manjari, Srikiran & Sarada

Sarangi, Rajasri

Sawhney, Om

Seth, Satish, Sadhana, Shilpa, Alpana & Ankur

Seth, Karan

Sharma, Om Prakash

Sharma, Shakuntala, Dr. Uma, Sandhya & Swati

Sharma, Sharvan, Indu, Versha & Neeraj

Sharma, Shyamala Narain, Sumitra Narain, Sandeep Narain, Anuj Narain & Vikas Narain

Sharma, Manmohan, Sushma, Ruby & Rina

Shukla, Sunil & Irene

Singh, Akhand, Usha, Amar & Ajai

Singh, Balvir, Ranjina, Shobna, Shalini & Abhinav

Singh, Dara & Jagit

Singh, Mukhtiar

Singh, Surendra P., Joyosree & Ratik

Sinha, Anjami

Soni, Usha, Rina, Moneka & Pankaj

Sran, Primajit Kaur

Srivastava, Brijbeheri

Subramanian, Gopalsamudram, Jayalakshmi, Krishnan & Sumitra

Subramanian, Lakshmi & Veena

Swaminathan, Indira, Anand, Padma & Ramya

Thachettu, Ivy

Thakur, Inder Hiralal, Priya Inder & Vishal Kiran

Thakur, Kanaya Metharam

Thampi, Vijaya

Thomas, Kurian, Molly, Vinod & Anita

Travasso, Alex, Anne, Lorraine & Lyon

Trivedi, Nirmal, Neeta & Parul

Tumkur, Chithralekha & Rammohan

Turlapati, Sanjay & Deepak

Uppal, Sukhwinder Kaur, Parminder Kaur & Kuldip Singh

Upreti, Dr. Gyan Chandra, Hema & Vikram

Vaid, Noshir

Vaz-Alexander, Juliet

Venkatesan, Geetha & Sukavanam

Venketeswaran, T.K.

Verma, Balwinder

Wadhawa, Serina & Akhil

Yallapragada, Gopala Krishna Murty

Yelevarthy, Dr. Nayudamma

ANNEX A

TERMS OF REFERENCE

Her Excellency the Governor General in Council, on the recommendation of the Prime Minister, hereby directs that a Commission do issue under Part I of the *Inquiries Act* and under the Great Seal of Canada appointing the Honourable John C. Major, Q.C., as Commissioner to conduct an inquiry into the investigation of the bombing of Air India Flight 182 (the "Inquiry"), which Commission shall direct

a. the Commissioner to conduct the Inquiry as he considers appropriate with respect to accepting as conclusive or giving weight to the findings of other examinations of the circumstances surrounding the bombing of Air India Flight 182, including

    i. the report of the Honourable Bob Rae entitled *Lessons to Be Learned* of November 23, 2005,

    ii. proceedings before the superior courts of British Columbia,

    iii. the 1991-1992 Security Intelligence Review Committee review of Canadian Security Intelligence Service activities in regard to the destruction of Air India Flight 182,

    iv. the report of the Honourable Mr. Justice B.N. Kirpal of the High Court of Delhi of February 26, 1986,

    v. the Aviation Occurrence Report of the Canadian Aviation Safety Board into the crash involving Air India Flight 182 of January 22, 1986,

    vi. the 1985 report of Blair Seaborn entitled *Security Arrangements Affecting Airports and Airlines in Canada*, and

vii.   the reports prepared by the Independent Advisory Panel assigned by the Minister of Transport to review the provisions of the *Canadian Air Transport Security Authority Act*, the operations of the Canadian Air Transport Security Authority and other matters relating to aviation security;

b.   the Commissioner to conduct the Inquiry specifically for the purpose of making findings and recommendations with respect to the following, namely,

i.   if there were deficiencies in the assessment by Canadian government officials of the potential threat posed by Sikh terrorism before or after 1985, or in their response to that threat, whether any changes in practice or legislation are required to prevent the recurrence of similar deficiencies in the assessment of terrorist threats in the future,

ii.   if there were problems in the effective cooperation between government departments and agencies, including the Canadian Security Intelligence Service and the Royal Canadian Mounted Police, in the investigation of the bombing of Air India Flight 182, either before or after June 23, 1985, whether any changes In practice or legislation are required to prevent the recurrence of similar problems of cooperation in the investigation of terrorism offences in the future,

iii.   the manner in which the Canadian government should address the challenge, as revealed by the investigation and prosecutions in the Air India matter, of establishing a reliable and workable relationship between security intelligence and evidence that can be used in a criminal trial,

      iv.   whether Canada's existing legal framework provides adequate constraints on terrorist financing in, from or through Canada, including constraints on the use or misuse of funds from charitable organizations,

      v.   whether existing practices or legislation provide adequate protection for witnesses against intimidation in the course of the investigation or prosecution of terrorism cases,

      vi.   whether the unique challenges presented by the prosecution of terrorism cases, as revealed by the prosecutions in the Air India matter, are adequately addressed by existing practices or legislation and, if not, the changes in practice or legislation that are required to address these challenges, including whether there is merit in having terrorism cases heard by a panel of three judges, and

      vii.   whether further changes in practice or legislation are required to address the specific aviation security breaches associated with the Air India Flight 182 bombing, particularly those relating to the screening of passengers and their baggage;

c.   the Commissioner to conduct the Inquiry under the name of the Commission of Inquiry into the Investigation of the Bombing of Air India Flight 182;

d.   that the Commissioner be authorized to adopt any procedures and methods that he may consider expedient for the proper conduct of the Inquiry, and to sit at any times and in any places in or outside Canada that he may decide;

e.   that the Commissioner be authorized to conduct consultations in relation to the Inquiry as he sees fit;

f.   that the Commissioner be authorized to grant to the families of the victims of the Air India Flight 182 bombing an opportunity for appropriate participation in the Inquiry;

g.   that the Commissioner be authorized to recommend to the Clerk of the Privy Council that funding be provided, in accordance with approved guidelines respecting rates of remuneration and reimbursement and the assessment of accounts, to ensure the appropriate participation of the families of the victims of the Air India Flight 182 bombing;

h.   that the Commissioner be authorized to grant to any other person who satisfies him that he or she has a substantial and direct interest in the subject-matter of the Inquiry an opportunity for appropriate participation in the Inquiry;

i.   that the Commissioner be authorized to recommend to the Clerk of the Privy Council that funding be provided, in accordance with approved guidelines respecting rates of remuneration and reimbursement and the assessment of accounts, to ensure the appropriate participation of any party granted standing under paragraph (h), to the extent of the party's interest, where in the Commissioner's view the party would not otherwise be able to participate in the Inquiry;

j.   that the Commissioner be authorized to rent any space and facilities that may be required for the purposes of the Inquiry, in accordance with Treasury Board policies;

k.   the Commissioner to use the automated litigation support program specified by the Attorney General of Canada and to rely, to the greatest extent possible, on documents that have been previously identified for use in Canadian criminal proceedings arising from the bombing of Air India Flight 182, and to consult with records management officials within the Privy Council Office on the use of standards and systems that are specifically designed for the purpose of managing records;

l.   that the Commissioner be authorized to engage the services of any experts and other persons referred to in section 11 of the *Inquiries Act*, at rates of remuneration and reimbursement approved by the Treasury Board;

m. the Commissioner, in conducting the Inquiry, to take all steps necessary to prevent disclosure of information which, if it were disclosed, could, in the opinion of the Commissioner, be injurious to international relations, national defence or national security and to conduct the proceedings in accordance with the following procedures, namely,

   i. on the request of the Attorney General of Canada, the Commissioner shall receive information *in camera* and in the absence of any party and their counsel if, in the opinion of the Commissioner, the disclosure of that information could be injurious to international relations, national defence or national security,

   ii. the Commissioner may release a part or a summary of the information received *in camera*, if, in the opinion of the Commissioner, its disclosure would not be injurious to international relations, national defence or national security, and shall provide the Attorney General of Canada with an opportunity to make submissions regarding international relations, national defence or national security prior to any release of a part or a summary of information received *in camera*,

   iii. if the Commissioner concludes that, contrary to the submissions of the Attorney General of Canada referred to in subparagraph (ii), disclosure of a part or a summary of information received *in camera* would not be injurious to international relations, national defence or national security, he shall so notify the Attorney General of Canada, which notice shall constitute notice under section 38.0 of the *Canada Evidence Act*,

   iv. the Commissioner shall provide the Attorney General of Canada with an opportunity to make submissions regarding international relations, national defence or national security with respect to any reports that are intended for release to the public prior to submitting such reports to the Governor in Council, and

    v.   if the Commissioner concludes that, contrary to the submissions of the Attorney General of Canada referred to in subparagraph (iv), disclosure of information contained in reports intended for release to the public would not be injurious to international relations, national defence or national security, he shall so notify the Attorney General of Canada, which notice shall constitute notice under section 38.01 of the *Canada Evidence Act*;

n. that nothing in that Commission shall be construed as limiting the application of the provisions of the *Canada Evidence Act*;

o. the Commissioner to follow established security procedures, including the requirements of the *Government Security Policy*, with respect to persons engaged pursuant to section 11 of the *Inquiries Act* and the handling of information at all stages of the Inquiry;

p. the Commissioner to perform his duties without expressing any conclusion or recommendation regarding the civil or criminal liability of any person or organization;

q. the Commissioner to perform his duties in such a way as to ensure that the conduct of the Inquiry does not jeopardize any ongoing criminal investigation or criminal proceeding;

r. the Commissioner to file the papers and records of the Inquiry with the Clerk of the Privy Council as soon as reasonably possible after the conclusion of the Inquiry;

s. the Commissioner to submit a report or reports, simultaneously in both official languages, to the Governor in Council; and

t. the Commissioner to ensure that members of the public can, simultaneously in both official languages, communicate with, and obtain services from it, including transcripts of proceedings if made available to the public.

ANNEX B

WITNESS LIST (Order of Appearances or Submissions)

WITNESSES	FAMILY MEMBERS REPRESENTED
September 25, 2006	
Dr. Bal Gupta	***Ramwati Gupta,*** *wife*
Lata Pada	***Vishnu Pada***, husband;
	Arti Pada, daughter;
	Brinda Pada, daughter
Deepak Khandelwal	***Chandra Khandelwal***, sister;
	Manju Khandelwal, sister
Satrajpal (Fred) Rai	***Kiranjit Rai***, cousin
Sundaram (Ramu) Ramakesavan	***Mukul Paliwal***, friend of family
September 26, 2006	
Kalwant Mamak	***Rajinder Mamak***, wife
Rama Bhardwaj	***Harish Bhardwaj***, son
Jayashree Thampi	***Kanaka Lakshmanan***, husband;
	Preethi Lakshmanan, daughter
Zerina Pai	***Noshir Vaid***, brother
Dr. Padmini Turlapati	***Sanjay Turlapati***, son;
	Deepak Turlapati, son
Susheel Gupta	***Ramwati Gupta***, mother
Jagada Venkateswaran	***Lakshmi Subramanian***, sister-in-law;
	Veena Subramanian, niece
Parkash Bedi	***Saroj Bedi***, wife;
	Anu Bedi, daughter;
	Jatin Bedi, son

September 27, 2006

Seanie Murphy   **Rescue and Recovery Workers**

Daniel Brown

Mark Tait

Mark Stagg

Thomas Hayes

September 28, 2006

Murthy Subramanian   *Lakshmi Subramanian*, wife;
                                Veena Subramanian, daughter

Esmie Alexander   *Anchanatt Mathew Alexander*,
                                husband

Lorna Kelly   *Barsa Kelly*, mother

Mansi Kinworthy   *Shashi Gupta*, mother

October 3, 2006

Monique Montpetit-Castonguay   *Rachelle Castonguay*, sister-in-law

Mahesh Chandra Sharma   *Uma Sharma*, wife;
                                Shakuntala Sharma, mother-in-law;
                                Swati Sharma, daughter;
                                Sandhya Sharma, daughter

Rob Alexander   *Anchanatt Mathew Alexander*, father

Dr. Anita Gupta   *Anumita Gupta*, sister

Krishna Bhat   *Muktha Bhat*, wife;
                                Deepak Bhat, son

October 4, 2006

The Honourable Bob Rae

Promode Sabharwal — **Meghana Sabharwal**, daughter

Dr. Chandra Vaidyanathan — **Krishnakumar Gopalan**, brother

Vipin Bery — **Neelam Bery**, wife; **Aditya Bery**; son; **Priya Bery**, daughter

Perviz Madon — **Sam Madon**, husband

Natasha Madon — **Sam Madon**, father

Eric Beauchesne — **Gaston Beauchesne**, father

Dr. and Mrs. Ramji Khandelwal — **Chandra Khandelwal**, daughter; **Manju Khandelwal**, daughter

October 5, 2006

Aleem Quraishi — **Shaiesta Quadri**, sister; **Qutubuddin Quadri**, brother-in-law; **Rubina Quadri**, niece; **Arishiya Quadri**, niece; **Atif Quadri**, nephew

Shipra Rana — **Shyla Aurora**, sister

Renee Saklikar — **Umar Jethwa**, uncle; **Zebunnisa Jethwa**, aunt

Banu Saklikar — **Umar Jethwa**, brother-in-law; **Zebunnisa Jethwa**, sister

Surjit Kalsi — **Indira Kalsi**, cousin

Smita Bailey	*Uma Sharma*, aunt;
	Shakuntala Sharma, grandmother;
	Swati Sharma, cousin;
	Sandhya Sharma, cousin
Mukta Laforte	*Uma Sharma*, aunt;
	Shakuntala Sharma, grandmother;
	Swati Sharma, cousin;
	Sandhya Sharma, cousin
Usha Sharma	*Uma Sharma*, sister;
	Shakuntala Sharma, mother;
	Swati Sharma, niece;
	Sandhya Sharma, niece
Asha Sharma, Ila Sharma and	*Uma Sharma*, sister;
Rama Sharma	*Shakuntala Sharma*, mother;
	Swati Sharma, niece;
	Sandhya Sharma, niece
Shridhar Sharma	*Uma Sharma*, sister-in-law;
	Shakuntala Sharma, mother-in-law;
	Swati Sharma, niece;
	Sandhya Sharma, niece
Romesh and Irene Kachroo	*Mohan Kachroo*, mother and mother-in-law
Vijay Kachru	*Mohan Kachroo*, mother
Meera Kachroo	*Mohan Kachroo*, grandmother

October 10, 2006

Donna Ramah Paul	*Vinubhai Bhatt*;
	Chandrabala Bhatt;
	Bina Bhatt;
	Tina Bhatt

Nicola Kelly	**Barsa Kelly**, mother
Upendrakumar Abda	**Chandrabala Bhatt**, sister;
	Vinubhai Bhatt, brother-in-law;
	Bina Bhatt, niece;
	Tina Bhatt, niece
Ramachandran Gopalan	**Krishnakumar Gopalan**, brother
Mohammad Irfan Umar Jethwa	**Umar Jethwa**, father;
	Zebunnisa Jethwa, mother
Mandip Singh Grewal	**Daljit Singh Grewal**, father
Shailendra Gupta	**Shashi Gupta**, wife;
	Suman Khera, sister-in-law;
	Rashi Khera, niece
Shobha Dewan	**Shashi Gupta**, sister;
	Suman Khera, sister;
	Rashi Khera, niece
Gaurav Gupta	**Shashi Gupta**, mother;
	Suman Khera, aunt;
	Rashi Khera, cousin

October 11, 2006

Dr. Haranhalli Radhakrishna	**Nagasundara Radhakrishna**, wife;
	Thejus Radhakrishna, son;
	Jyothi Radhakrishna, daughter
Rattan Singh Kalsi	**Indira Kalsi**, daughter
Ann Venketeswaran	**T.K. Venketeswaran**, husband
Esther Venketeswaran	**T.K. Venketeswaran**, father
Chandar Sain Malhotra	**Atul K. Malholtra**, son

October 12, 2006

Krishna Sharma	***Om Prakash Sharma***, husband
Saroj Gaur	***Om Prakash Sharma***, father
Neelam Kaushik	***Om Prakash Sharma***, father
Veena Sharma	***Om Prakash Sharma***, father
Madhu Gaur	***Om Prakash Sharma***, father
Sheila Singh Hanse	***Narendra Singh Hanse***, husband
Swaran Singh Hanse	***Narendra Singh Hanse***, father-in-law
Anil Hanse	***Narendra Singh Hanse***, father
Sanjay Lazar	***Sampath Lazar***, father;
	Sylvia Lazar, stepmother;
	Sandeeta Lazar, stepsister
Laxmansinh Jayantkumar Abda	***Vinubhai Bhatt***, uncle;
	Chandrabala Bhatt, aunt;
	Bina Bhatt, cousin;
	Tina Bhatt, cousin

October 13, 2006

Amarjit Bhinder	***Satwinder Singh Bhinder***, husband
Tahir Sadiq	***Sugra Sadiq***, mother
Sheroo D. Dumasia	***Dara D. Dumasia***, husband
Ram Gogia	***Bhagwanti Gogia***, mother
Freny Enayati	***Ardeshir K. Enayati***, husband
Sandhya Nil Singh	***Surendra P. Singh***, brother;
	Joyosree Singh, sister-in-law;
	Ratik Singh, nephew

Ratheish Yelevarthy	**Nayudamma Yelevarthy**, father

November 7, 2006

Dianne Beauchesne	**Gaston Beauchesne**, father

June 18, 2007

Dr. Chandra Sankurathri	**Manjari Sankurathri**, wife; **Srikiran Sankurathri**, son; **Sarada Sankurathri**, daughter

ANNEX C

TIMELINE OF KEY EVENTS

Saturday, June 22, 1985

20:22 EDT (00:22 GMT)
CP Air Flight 060 from Vancouver arrives in Toronto. Some passengers and baggage transfer to Air India Flight 182.

17:37 PDT (00:37 GMT)
CP Air Flight 003 departs Vancouver for Tokyo.

21:02 EDT (01:02 GMT)
Air India Flight 182 arrives in Mirabel from Toronto after a delay of 1 hour 40 minutes; 105 additional passenger board the flight.

22:18 EDT (02:18 GMT)
Air India Flight 182 departs Mirabel bound for Heathrow in London UK.

Sunday, June 23, 1985

05:41 GMT
CP Air 003 arrives 14 minutes early at Narita Airport.

06:15 GMT
Explosion in the Narita Airport baggage terminal kills two and injures four.

07:14 GMT
Air India Flight 182, with 329 people on board, disappears from radar screens.

09:44 GMT
SOS broadcast in Ireland re an Air India jumbo jet going down.

10:02 GMT
Laurentian Forest arrives at the crash scene. There are no survivors.

Subsequent Events

June 26, 1985
India's Prime Minister Rajiv Gandhi writes Canada's Prime Minister Brian Mulroney about the disaster.

July 18, 1985
Prime Minister Mulroney writes letter to Prime Minister Gandhi to assure that Canada will identify and prosecute perpetrators if this is proven to be sabotage.

November 8, 1985
RCMP officers raid the homes of Talwinder Singh Parmar and Inderjit Singh Reyat in B. C. and lay various charges relating to weapons, explosives and conspiracy.

January 22, 1986
Canadian Aviation Safety Board determines a bomb brought down Air India Flight 182.

February 1988
Inderjit Singh Reyat is arrested in England and charged with making the bomb that exploded at Tokyo's Narita Airport.

December 13, 1989
Reyat is extradited to Canada.

May 10, 1991
Reyat is convicted of two counts of manslaughter and four explosives charges related to the Narita bomb and sentenced to ten years.

October 27, 2000
The RCMP arrest Ripudaman Singh Malik and Ajaib Singh Bagri in connection with the bombing of Air India Flight 182 and the Narita Airport bombing. Charges include 331 counts of first-degree murder.

June 4, 2001
RCMP arrest Reyat on seven new charges including murder, attempted murder, conspiracy in the Air India bombing, and the Narita explosion.

February 10, 2003
Reyat pleads guilty to one count of manslaughter and a charge of aiding in the construction of a bomb in relation to Air India Flight 182. All other charges against him are stayed and he is sentenced to five years in prison.

February 24, 2003
Crown and defence agree that the trial of Bagri and Malik will be presided over by a judge instead of judge and jury.

March 16, 2005
Malik and Bagri are acquitted of all charges.

March 16, 2005
Families of victims renew their call for a public inquiry.

April 26, 2005
Former Ontario Premier Bob Rae is appointed to advise the federal government on whether to call a public inquiry into the investigation and prosecution.

June 23, 2005
First appearance by a Canadian Prime Minister at the annual memorial service in Ahakista, Dunmanus Bay, Ireland.

November 23, 2005
Bob Rae's report recommends further inquiry into the Air India bombing, calling for a "focused, policy-based inquiry".

March 3, 2006
National Parole Board denies Reyat parole and rules that he must complete his prison sentence to 2008.

March 7, 2006
Prime Minister Stephen Harper asks retired Supreme Court Justice John Major to consult with the families of victims on the terms of reference for an inquiry.

May 1, 2006
Prime Minister Harper announces the establishment of an inquiry, led by the Hon. John Major, into the investigation of the Air India bombing to seek to find "answers to several key questions about the worst mass murder in Canadian history".

June 21, 2006
Official launch of the Commission of Inquiry into the Investigation of the Bombing of Air India Flight 182.

September 26-November 17, 2006
Commission hears family testimony as well as testimony from rescuers and Canadian officials in Ireland immediately after the bombing.

ANNEX D

PHOTO CAPTIONS

    1 Monument at Ahakista, Ireland (photo taken by the Turlapatis)
  2-5 Three Generations: Shakuntala, Uma, Sandhya and
       Swati Sharma
  6-7 Chandra and Manju Khandelwal
    8 Barsa Kelly
    9 Dr. Anchanatt Mathew Alexander
10-11 Nagasundara, Jyothi and Thejus Radhakrishna
12-13 The Quadris with Rubina and the Quadri children together
   14 Sanjay and Deepak Turlapati
15-16 Muktha and Deepak Bhat
   17 Tina Bhatt with her stethoscope
   18 Rachelle Castonguay
   19 Krishnakumar Gopalan graduating from Carleton University in
       Ottawa
   20 Krishnakumar's mother, Mrs. Thangam Gopalan
   21 Satwinder Singh Bhinder, co-captain of the *Kanishka*
   22 Gaston Beauchesne
   23 Lakshmi and Veena Subramanian
   24 Drs. Zebunnisa and Umar Jethwa prior to the flight at the
       Vancouver International Airport
   25 Narendra Singh Hanse, Captain of the *Kanishka*
   26 Sam Madon
   27 Bhagwanti Gogia and family members
   28 "Nana" Kachroo
   29 Om Prakash Sharma
   30 The Arun Lifeboat
   31 Mark Stagg - Jana Chytilova / The Vancouver Sun
   32 Laurentian Forest
   33 Another view of the Laurentian Forest
   34 A Sea King helicopter
   35 Map of Ireland
   36 The Turlaptis and friends at dinner in Ireland
37-39 Saroj, Anu and Jatin Bedi
40-42 Shashi Gupta, Suman Khera and Rashi Khera

ANNEX E

COMMISSION STAFF (staff and consultants engaged by the Commission at the time of this report)

Commissioner's Office
Major, Hon. John C. –Commissioner
Kenny, Barbara

Registrar
Brisson, Gilles

Administration
Brook, Dennis –Director-Operations
Cooke, Lynne –Director-Finance
Ariano, Wanda
Brisson, Richard
Duquette, Julie
Godbout, Gail
Hooper, Anne
Karmali, Nadia
Monette, Pierre
Mutton, Mary
Osborne, Anita
Rock, Stéphanie
Snedden, Paul
Surprenant, Roland
Thomas, Roger

Research

Archambault, Peter –Director-Research

Roach, Kent –Director-Legal Research

Archdeacon, Maurice

Dickerson, Ken

Media and Communications

Tansey, Michael

Editorial and Report Production

Gussman, Tom –Senior Editor

Sadinsky, Ian –Senior Editor

Fitzsimmons, Donna - Design and Production

Cremer, Pierre - Translation

Drolet, Daniel

Lutes, Kimberley

Legal

Freiman, Mark –Commission Lead Counsel

Dorval, Michel –Co-counsel

Kapoor, Anil

Gover, Brian

Bilodeau, Roger

Barragan, Francis

Blum, Nadine

Boucher, Alexandre

Bowes, Tanya

Carle, Frédéric

Coutlée, Geneviève

Dosanjh, Arpal